Contemporary Management Accounting Practices in UK Manufacturing

David Dugdale
Department of Accounting and Finance
University of Bristol

Colwyn Jones
School of Sociology
University of the West of England, Bristol

Stephen Green
Business School
Group Limited

ELSEVIER

AMSTERDAM • BOSTON • HEIDELBERG • LONDON
NEW YORK • OXFORD • PARIS • SAN DIEGO
SAN FRANCISCO • SINGAPORE • SYDNEY • TOKYO

CIMA Publishing is an imprint of Elsevier

CIMA
PUBLISHING

CIMA Publishing
An imprint of Elsevier
Linacre House, Jordan Hill, Oxford OX2 8DP
30 Corporate Drive, Burlington, MA 01803

First published 2006

British Library Cataloguing in Publication Data
A catalogue record for this book is available from the British Library

Library of Congress Cataloguing in Publication Data
A catalogue record for this book is available from the Library of Congress

ISBN-10:   0-7506-6871-7
ISBN-13:   978-0-7506-6871-2

For information on all CIMA Publishing Publications
visit our website at www.cimapublishing.com

Typeset by Integra Software Services Pvt. Ltd, Pondicherry, India
www.integra-india.com
Printed and bound in Great Britain

06   07   08   09   10   10 9 8 7 6 5 4 3 2 1

Working together to grow
libraries in developing countries

www.elsevier.com | www.bookaid.org | www.sabre.org

ELSEVIER   BOOK AID
International   Sabre Foundation

To Andrew and Ang

Contents

Executive Summary

Contemporary Practices in UK Manufacturing Accounting – a CIMA research project – reveals methods currently used for reporting financial information in UK manufacturing companies. Based on 41 companies, it shows a rich diversity of reporting practices that are constrained neither by the financial accounting requirements of SSAP9 nor by any sense of general management accounting trends. Instead, Financial Directors choose from a toolkit of "traditional" and "contemporary" practices in constructing reporting systems appropriate to their varied commercial needs, but with a strong leaning towards *contribution margin* approaches. These choices cover a wide range of reporting practices in relation to contribution, margin, profit, variances, budgets and forecasts.

Research methods

This book deals with the presentation and analysis of financial information in the 41 UK manufacturing companies. The research was stimulated by a previous investigation that unexpectedly revealed that a number of manufacturing companies present financial information in contribution format rather than in the "gross margin" style consistent with financial reporting requirements. A pilot study confirmed that a number of companies use contribution statements in their internal financial reporting. However, initial company visits also revealed considerable variation in terminology and much scope for misinterpretation of practice. To combat this, companies participating in the main study were asked to provide pro forma Profit and Loss (P&L) accounts and these were analysed and provided the basis for follow-up structured interviews. The pro forma P&L formats together with short summaries of practice and company overviews are set out in the Appendix (supplied on CD) to this report.

Our *document-based interviewing* method has a number of advantages. First, the information presented is likely to be faithful to reporting practice in participating companies at the time of the study. Respondents were invited to check the interview summaries and discussion in the main report can be checked against the P&L

layouts and summaries in the Appendix. Second, the combination of documentary evidence and interviews helps avoid inferring researchers' meanings rather than those actually intended by practitioners. Third, where interesting accounting methods are adopted in companies, these could be pursued and set out in greater depth.

The disadvantage of *document-based interviewing* is the commitment required from firms and only about 9% of companies contacted were willing to participate in the study. Thus, validity is achieved at the expense of representativeness but, in our view, the results strongly justify this trade-off.

Costing techniques

The study reveals that virtually all the techniques developed since the late nineteenth century, and evident in the historical literature, are still in use today. There are examples of "traditional" techniques such as absorption costing, standard costing and marginal costing as well as "contemporary" techniques such as activity-based costing and throughput accounting. New techniques are often marketed by denigrating existing methods, identifying them as "problems" before unveiling new techniques as the "solution". For example, standard costing was once hailed as more effective and much less expensive than the "job-order cost plans" of the early twentieth century. Direct costing was sold as simpler and more informative than absorption costing. Activity-based costing promised to be more accurate and to avoid the misleading signals of traditional costing methods. However, "old" methods have not died: they are still taught, examined and used.

Prevalence of contribution statements in internal financial reporting

In the report, participating companies are broadly categorised as "contribution companies" or "gross margin companies". This was not easy because of ubiquitous references within companies to "gross profit", "gross margin" and "manufacturing margin" applied to P&L lines that textbooks would refer to as "contribution margin". However, we conclude that 28 (approximately 68%) of the survey companies employ contribution statements. All these companies treat material cost as variable and 21 companies (75%) treat labour as a variable cost. Other "variable" costs appear less frequently: variable production overhead in 12 companies; transport/distribution costs in 7 companies and variable selling costs in 3 companies.

Prevalence of standard costing but limited variance analysis

Most (29) of the 41 companies employ standard costs and, of those that do not, 8 have only limited manufacturing operations or are engaged in contract work. Therefore only 4 companies (less than 10%) do not employ standard costing where this might be expected. All (29) "standard costing companies" set standards for materials, most (26) set standards for labour and about two-thirds (20) set overhead recovery rates. However, standard cost variances often do not appear as part of P&L information. Over half of these "standard cost companies" base P&L reports on actual costs; some "add back" variances while others frequently update material standards so that they approximate actual costs.

Although not necessarily appearing in the P&L, most of these companies calculate some material and labour variances for control purposes. Overhead variances are less prevalent and only one company reports subdivisions of both variable and fixed overhead variances. No company subdivides the fixed overhead volume variance into capacity and efficiency elements. Variance reporting is therefore very selective.

Inter-relationships between financial presentation and costing systems

Financial reporting presentation and costing methods are inter-related and most of the 28 "contribution companies" make a P&L adjustment for "overhead in stock" that allows "bottom line" P&L to be reported on a full cost basis. Surprisingly, 11 of these "contribution companies" establish "full" standard costs in order to value stock consistent with financial reporting requirements. In these companies a contribution orientation is *loosely coupled* with a full standard cost system. In "gross margin" companies, systems are usually more *tightly coupled*: 7 companies adopt a gross margin approach and, consistently, adopt full standard costing.

Contribution companies can trace variable costs to products or product groups and, in some companies, this analysis provides the starting point for further analysis of segment profitability, attributing overhead to products, markets or distribution channels. This is reminiscent of activity-based ideas and several companies had experience of activity-based costing, usually intended to establish more accurate product costs. However, although one-off ABC exercises had provided some valuable insights, none of the survey companies were currently using the technique.

Choice of financial reporting and costing systems

Senior managers could influence the choice of policy and it was clear that, in some companies, the finance director or financial controller had sufficient influence to determine the choice of system. The choices of these managers were influenced by their experiences and two senior managers ensured that conservative (marginal) methods were employed for stock valuation. Financial controllers tended to prefer marginal methods because of their simplicity and utility. In several companies, parent company policies could be very important either directly or through their influence on technology choice; several companies had harmonised their systems with the wider group and/or planned to update their MRP systems. The nationality of the parent company could also be a factor and, for example, we noted some similarity in the reporting adopted by companies under Gallic ownership.

Budgeting and forecasting

All but one of the companies sets budgets and reports budget variances and most companies make regular forecasts. Most forecasts are for the financial year, typically referred to as, for example, "3 + 9" or "6 + 6" forecasts. The concentration on financial year reporting reveals the influence of external pressures and, at one company, current and previous year results are compared: ". . .

because that's the way the stock market seems to work". One company is exceptional in developing its forecasts to include the remainder of the current financial year and the whole of the following year. This development, including innovative graphical presentations, is set out in detail in the Appendix.

Incentive schemes

Most of the companies operate either executive or staff incentive schemes and 13 operate both.

The executive schemes have a heavy reliance on financial performance measures and over half of the companies (10 from 18) use profit versus budget or target in their schemes. The most important non-financial item in these schemes is "personal performance".

The staff schemes also rely heavily on financial measures. Although non-financial measures such as on-time delivery, customer feedback and quality are occasionally employed, relatively few companies use these measures.

About half of all incentive schemes are based on a single performance measure. The remainder use combinations of measures and, in a few schemes, there are as many as four measures in combination. Although financial measures are prevalent these are not particularly sophisticated, only three of the executive schemes use return on capital employed and none use residual income or its more modern version, economic value added.

The "relevance lost" debate

A loud critique of management accounting over the last 20 or so years is that it has lost its managerial relevance through subservience to the requirements of external financial accounting. If so, in the UK, this would mean that SSAP9 acts as a strong constraint on internal financial reporting. This survey undermines this view. Instead, we find a wide range of practices that are constructed in response to the particular commercial circumstances of individual companies and *not* imposed by an external financial accounting regime. Thus there are very varied practices in UK manufacturing companies. The survey companies employ:

marginal costing and contribution ideas;
standard costing but often combined with reports based on actual costs;
variance analysis but limited use of overhead variances;
segmental reporting;
budgeting, forecasting and incentive schemes.

Companies have a wide range of options in order to ensure that their systems are "relevant" and the majority of the survey companies had opted for direct or marginal costing.

The number of companies employing contribution methods and, to a greater or lesser extent, marginal costing, suggests that manufacturing companies in general are *not* dominated by the (full cost) requirements of financial reporting standards. However, matters are not quite this simple. We note that the *bottom line* P&L in most companies is reported in accordance with SSAP9 and although, technically, it is easy to report *both* marginal and full cost P&L, only one company does this. Additionally, companies employ cycles of budgeting and forecasting that are clearly influenced by external financial reporting requirements. We conclude that, in many companies, financial reporting does not lead to the inappropriate use of full product costs. However, internal financial reporting is often influenced by external reporting cycles, and managers are conscious of the need to meet external expectations.

Issues for reflection

There is considerable interest in contribution analysis in the companies studied. Although there has been a widespread presumption that absorption costing systems dominate manufacturing practice this study reveals that companies often follow long-standing academic advice in structuring their internal P&L reporting on contribution lines. However, the analysis is sometimes not very systematic – for example, only one company derives *both* marginal and full cost profit on a month-to-month basis. There is scope for the more systematic application of marginal cost principles and contribution reporting.

Manufacturing companies usually employ standard costing systems. However, they tend to be selective in their use of variance analysis, and analysis of overhead variances was very limited. These practices may reflect the widespread criticism that the (mis)use of variance analysis has received, especially in JIT and TQM environments. Companies using variance analysis need to be aware of the limitations of the technique.

Interviewees were generally very conscious of the arguments for and against the apportionment and allocation of overhead to cost objects such as divisions, responsibility centres, products and services. However, some companies employed quite sophisticated segmental profitability analysis based on the thoughtful attribution of overhead. This was especially so in contribution companies because the contribution line provides a sound starting point for such analysis. Companies adopting contribution style presentations can add value to the presentation by identifying levels of contribution. Contribution calculated after variable costs and after sales and marketing costs by market, distribution channel or customer can be especially valuable for some companies.

There is extensive use of budgeting, forecasting and incentive schemes but the methods adopted are, typically, relatively unsophisticated. For example, most companies make forecasts only at the end of the financial year and employ a very limited range of performance criteria in their incentive schemes. Forecasting systems could be extended so that a rolling twelve-month forecast is routinely available and further research into the design, use and impact of incentive schemes would be desirable.

Introduction

Following the publication of Johnson and Kaplan's (1987) critique of management accounting in which they claimed that, in the US case, management accounting had long lost its relevance for management decision making, there has been considerable academic interest in the development and diffusion of "new" management accounting theories and practices. The original critique was stimulated by an analysis that identified a deep malaise in US industry that meant it was struggling in the face of an unprecedented wave of new opportunities and threats in a "new manufacturing environment" (Armstrong, 2002; Jones and Dugdale, 2002). American manufacturing was portrayed as increasingly located in a global market, under challenge from international (especially Japanese) competitors, and failing to make effective use of new management techniques and advanced manufacturing technology. The analysis identified the cause of the malaise in inadequate or misleading management information resting on a failure of managerial expertise, and of calculative expertise in particular (Miller and O'Leary, 1993) leading to a crisis of confidence in management accounting (Dent, 1990).

Originally this thesis was specifically related to US manufacturing, but it quickly became generalized to other countries and organisations, and the 1990s saw a busy marketplace for a wide variety of new management accounting theories and practices. In part this was fuelled by expansion of management consulting activity with consultants being hungry for new accounting packages to market to managers uncertain about the efficacy of their existing accounting systems. For example, PricewaterhouseCoopers and KPMG promoted Activity-based Costing/Management (ABC/ABM), Stern Stewart trademarked Economic Value Added as EVA™, and the Goldratt Institute produced Throughput Accounting (TA).[1] Each promised an holistic approach to reforming accounting systems to provide more accurate and/or more relevant information for management.

The adoption of such new accounting forms was tracked by a series of questionnaire surveys that showed, by the early 1990s, around 20% of the largest UK companies claiming to have

---

[1]The latter usually referred to in the UK as Theory of Constraints in accounting.

implemented ABC systems (Innes and Mitchell, 1995b). This figure rose to 60% when those claiming intentions to experiment with ABC were included, with a further 40% of UK firms claiming to be using, or planning to use, TA (Bright *et al.*, 1992). This would appear to indicate widespread innovation in UK business. There are, however, some doubts about the meaning and validity of these claims and Bright *et al.* note that the figures produced by their questionnaire:

> did not conform to our own observations . . . [and] many managers were willing to debate the advantages and disadvantages of different "advanced" techniques and practices with only a very tentative understanding of what the terms embraced and involved. (1992, p. 204)

Thus practitioners' claims to be using new techniques need to be treated with caution and documentary evidence is important in confirming; first, that such techniques are actually in use and, secondly, the nature of these techniques.

Another issue is problematic in researching "contemporary" accounting practice with its implication that contemporary practice differs from previous practice. Typically, new developments are accompanied by doubts about whether anything on offer is really "new". The introduction of ABC in the late 1980s could be seen as a reformulation of the "functional costing" that had appeared in Longman and Schiff's (1955) *Practical Distribution Cost Analysis* (Horngren, quoted in Robinson, 1990: p. 23). Similarly EVA™ may be seen as a variety of the "residual income" approach; and TA as a rediscovery of "contribution-per-unit-of-limiting-factor". Thus "new" management accounting systems might recycle long-standing theories and practices having their origins far back into the twentieth century. Armstrong claims that the argumentation style of those proposing management accounting systems typically involves appeals to managerial common sense – drawing upon what is already known – and thus these systems must reflect what is already accepted: "It is mode of evolution in which innovation consists of catching up with what business commonsense already 'knows'" (1995, p. 16). Certainly the debates between rival supporters of the absorption costing version of ABC and the direct costing of TA in the 1980s and 1990s rehearsed arguments that were well covered in similar battles between absorption costers and direct costers in the UK in the 1950s and 1960s (Dugdale and Jones, 2003). These, in turn, echoed disputes in the early years of the century. Garcke and Fells' (1887) textbook advocated a form of what, today, would be identified as "marginal" costing (Boyns and Edwards, 1997a) but in the textbooks of the 1920s and 1930s it was absorption costing that had acquired theoretical hegemony (Glover and Williams, 1928; Wheldon, 1937; Carter, 1938). Many of today's "new" management accounting practices may thus be seen as "re-inventing the wheel".

One might ask, then, what to count as innovation in management accounting? The verb "to innovate" may be defined as "to introduce as something new" (Chambers Dictionary). *Absolute innovation* may thus be seen as the introduction of something that has not existed before; something entirely novel. At one extreme, such novelty might be defined as a fundamental departure from pre-existing accounting theories and practices but, if so, then it may be impossible to discover any such "paradigm shift" (Kuhn, 1962) in management accounting. Indeed, Kuhn (1970) himself doubts whether such paradigm analysis can be applied in the social sciences and, in this respect, we may find management accounting to conform with this pattern. At the other extreme, if any repackaging or relabelling of existing accounting is taken as innovatory, then minor or cosmetic amendment may be mistaken for significant substantive change. However, for accountants and managers who are actually engaged in changing their accounting systems, such distinctions may not be highly relevant. Instead, what is of significance is *relative innovation* in which practitioners are introducing different systems that are new in relation to the recent experiences of either the individuals or of the companies involved. In designing and implementing such systems in the particular contexts of current circumstances such individuals and companies are innovating – regardless of whether other individuals and companies, in different circumstances, have followed similar paths before. In addition to such changes, some of what may be regarded as innovation may properly be seen as practices that diverge from those expected even though they may have been in place in particular companies for some time. They are in this sense new to the observer, even if they are familiar to the practitioner. All of these conceptions of innovation have informed our study of contemporary management accounting practices.

The study was stimulated by exploratory work in six companies where the initial focus was upon approaches to pricing and the roles of management accountants and marketers in pricing decisions. This involved investigation of internal reporting processes because of the potential interaction between costs, margins and prices. To the researchers' surprise it was clear that internal reporting in some of the companies visited had undergone significant change in recent years. First, none of the companies placed much emphasis on the calculation or reporting of variances against production cost standards. And, second, three of the six companies did not adopt the traditional profit and loss format. Instead of deducting cost of sales from revenue to establish gross margin they deducted production variable costs and market/ business segment related costs to establish "contribution" from each business unit or segment. Manufacturing and general overhead was then deducted in order to establish net profit.

In one innovative company both activity-based *and* throughput ideas had been integrated into standard internal reporting. The managing director of the company referred to throughput (although he could not remember where he heard the term) defining it as sales less material cost of sales. "Throughput" was calculated for each business sector and then marketing and directly attributable, transaction related, product and customer costs were deducted to establish "segmental contribution". This seemed rather sophisticated, combining the reporting of activity-based transaction-related costs (in marketing and distribution) with ideas from throughput accounting. The internal reports reflected the company's new organisation structure by providing information to the managers responsible for sales in the two key business segments. Nevertheless the managing director of the company was still dissatisfied with the management accounting system. His latest intent was to develop a more dynamic set of reporting standards drawing ideas from the "beyond budgeting" and "throughput" literatures. The accounting practices adopted in this company, and those observed in the other companies during the exploratory research, led to the identification of manufacturing accounting innovation as an important issue for investigation. If the innovatory practices found in the small sample of companies were widespread, then it would be evidence of a rehabilitation of management accounting following Johnson and Kaplan's (1987) charge of *Relevance Lost* – or, possibly, that this charge was never plausible in the UK.

This monograph reports the *CIMA Contemporary Practices in UK Manufacturing Accounting* project.[2] The aim of the project was to investigate internal management accounting reports in UK manufacturing companies. The study investigated whether the development of new theory-based techniques, changes in organizational contexts, differing perceptions, values and interests of management accountants, and other factors have led to change in the presentation of financial information.

The project had three specific objectives:

1. to investigate whether internal management accounting policies and reporting are currently dominated by the requirements of financial reporting;
2. to establish the *nature* of innovatory forms of management information and begin to explore *where* and *why* they have been introduced;
3. to disseminate innovative practice in management accounting.

The research disclosed a highly varied range of practices in companies. Whilst the external influences of financial reporting, through auditing and in anticipation of International Accounting Standards, was present, it did not dominate management information. Rather than the traditional absorption costing that might be anticipated in manufacturing, the use of contribution margin was found to be widespread. Although the availability of computer software accounting practices might suggest some degree of standardization, the particular practices adopted varied considerably between companies that differed in terms of their products, production methods, markets and forms of ownership – with the impact of foreign ownership being marked. The adoption of such

---

[2]Originally titled the *CIMA Innovation in Manufacturing Accounts* project. The title was eventually changed so that readers would not be misled as to the content of the report.

practices was rarely influenced by management consultants and, instead, represented individual decisions within companies that were heavily influenced by the personal experiences and preferences of key managers and accountants. Hence, accounting practices were generated and reproduced through varied social action in varied social contexts. This means that, other than a general interest in contribution accounting, there is no clear direction or "evolution" of manufacturing accounting practice. Indeed, in some cases, one company may be adopting a particular practice at the same moment that another is abandoning it. What the companies hold generally in common, however, is that they have room for manoeuvre in determining their management accounting practices, since these are not dictated by financial reporting requirements.

The remaining chapters of this report are structured as follows:

- ◆ Chapter 2 reviews research into the development of management accounting, prescriptions for new forms of accounting, and surveys of contemporary practice.
- ◆ Chapter 3 lays out the methods employed in studying the 41 companies.
- ◆ Chapter 4 reports the Profit & Loss Account reporting conventions adopted.
- ◆ Chapter 5 deals with the nature and use of costing and variance analysis.
- ◆ Chapter 6 deals with issues of integrating the techniques discussed in the previous two chapters.
- ◆ Chapter 7 covers the treatment of overhead costs.
- ◆ Chapter 8 covers budgets, forecasts, performance measurement and reward.
- ◆ Chapter 9 draws together our overview of contemporary forms of manufacturing accounting.
- ◆ Chapter 10 concludes with a review of the theoretical and practical implications of our study for researchers and practitioners.

Literature Review and Historical Context

2.1 Introduction

Much of our analysis will deal with cost accounting practices in the 41 companies investigated. These practices include absorption costing, marginal costing, standard costing, activity-based costing, budgeting and forecasting. It seems that virtually all cost accounting practices can be found if one looks hard enough. This observation leads us to the view that most of the body of cost and management accounting theory is relevant to this research project. We therefore provide an overview of historical developments in the subject, showing how new ideas have been justified, compared and contrasted with older ideas and integrated into a growing body of theory.

In Section 2.2 we trace costing history in the UK although, because of mutual influences, there are inevitable references to the US. We briefly mention the origin of techniques such as absorption costing, standard costing, direct (marginal) costing and relevant costing and summarise the main features of each innovation. The historical perspective shows how new ideas have promised advance over existing methods, but, instead of the pre-existing methods being swept away by superior techniques, each innovation has been added to the mounting body of theory. Our field study shows that *all* the techniques become available as a "toolkit" that can be employed depending on context, circumstance and individual experience.

The historical Section 2.2, includes critiques of "traditional" methods by supporters of "new" techniques and reference to the debates between supporters of "established" and "new" procedures. In Section 2.3, we review the contemporary critique of "traditional" methods and show how old controversies flared anew as proponents of throughput accounting and ABC debated the merits of their respective proposals. Finally, in Section 2.4, we review management accounting studies in the 1990s in order to gauge apparent usage of "old" techniques and the take up of "new" ideas.

Any recent management accounting history is now inescapably influenced by Johnson and Kaplan's (1987) "relevance lost" view of cost accounting history. Johnson and Kaplan claim that the nineteenth-century costing provided managers with useful information and the late nineteenth and early twentieth centuries saw further theoretical development with Church's sophisticated costing system and the development of standard costing and budgeting. However, by about 1925, Johnson and Kaplan claim that development had come to a halt as cost accounting became increasingly dominated by the requirements of financial accounting. A great opportunity was missed in the 1960s as the designers of computer-based systems simply automated the existing (financial accounting dominated) costing systems. And, by the 1980s, cost accounting systems, typically based on the absorption of manufacturing overhead on labour hour or cost bases, were seriously misleading (American) managers in an increasingly competitive and deregulated global marketplace. Our reading suggests that the Johnson and Kaplan "financial accounting dominance" and "cost accounting stagnation" models cannot be applied in the UK and we attempt to draw this out in the next section.

We believe there are important insights to be gained from a historical analysis, relevant to practices in the companies in our field study. However, readers who do not share this view can skip the next section and move to the 1980s critique and consequent surveys of practice.

2.2   A brief history of costing

Factory accounts

A number of authors such as Boyns and Edwards (1997a, b) have undertaken archival research that suggests that quite sophisticated costing methods were employed by companies during the industrial revolution. However, relatively little was written on the subject until the late nineteenth century when there was an upsurge of interest that Solomons (1952: 17) termed the "costing renaissance".

The "rebirth" of costing theory is usually traced to Garcke and Fells' (1887) Factory Accounts, the first important British textbook on cost accounting. Garcke and Fells were practical men and almost certainly had experience of the factory accounting system they describe. They proposed what would now be seen as an integrated system of factory and financial accounting and, exceptionally, appeared to favour a form of "direct" or "marginal" costing: "The establishment expenses and interest on capital should not . . . form part of the cost of production. There is no advantage in distributing these items over the various transactions or articles produced. They do not vary proportionately with the volume of business" (Garcke and Fells, 1893: 73).

Close reading of Garcke and Fells, however, reveals that matters are not quite so straightforward. Their detailed recommendation was that all manufacturing costs be attributed to jobs (including those that we would now usually regard as "fixed"): ". . . a more efficient check upon the indirect expenses would be obtained by establishing a relation between them and the direct expenses. This may be done by distributing all the indirect expenses, such as wages of foremen, rent of the factory, fuel, lighting, heating, and cleaning, &c. (but not the salaries of clerks, office rent, stationery and other establishment charges . . .), over the various jobs, as a percentage, either upon the jobs respectively, or upon the cost of both wages and materials" (p. 71). It is therefore possible to read Garcke and Fells as advocating both variable costing (in principle) but setting out the "full" absorption of factory costs (in practice).

The major contribution of Garcke and Fells was in showing how factory accounts for labour, materials (and overhead) could be constructed and integrated with the financial books of account. However, in the UK, despite this advocacy, the cost accounts and financial accounts were usually maintained separately. And a system of accounts based on direct or marginal costing had to wait for almost half a century before it received powerful advocacy. Early theorists concerned themselves with absorption costing and with whether the absorption of manufacturing cost should be separated from non-manufacturing cost.

Separating manufacturing from non-manufacturing costs

Garner (1954: 127) describes debates in the US where some felt that *all* costs should be traced to product, while others, such as Halsey, argued that the "cost of production" should exclude expenses incurred "outside the shop door". The matter was resolved in favour of separate analysis and by 1910: ". . . even A. Hamilton Church [who earlier took the former view] subscribed to the fundamental distinction . . ." (Garner, 1954: 137). A crucial difference in the treatment of manufacturing and non-manufacturing costs had become generally accepted.

Development of absorption costing theory

Early theoretical development focussed on absorption costing. Church was a key figure in these early developments publishing ". . . a series of articles . . . in 1901, [which] . . . developed his later famous 'scientific production center' technique for allocating burden items" (Garner, 1954: 187). Church set out detailed procedures for calculating "scientific machine hour rates" in *Factory Management: Manufacturing Costs and Accounts* (Church, 1917). Indirect expenses (depreciation, repairs, supervision, power, etc.) were to be identified by department and allocated directly to machines/ machine groups or accumulated against "production factors" such as buildings, power, supervision, organisation, etc. These "factor" costs could then be apportioned to machines/machine groups using bases such as space, horse power, etc. Finally the total cost attributed to each machine/machine group was divided by an estimate of available machine hours to yield machine hour rates (Church, 1917: 66). These absorption costing principles have now been practised for over a century.[3]

Church's recommendations were also "modern" in his advocacy that machine hour rates be based, not on actual costs expended and machine hours worked, but on *normal* expense and capacity levels. Suppose plant is running at less than normal capacity, then he asks ". . . would it be wise to quote $1,230 for the work? The answer is obvious. If we did so, we should lose the order" (p. 72). So Church recommended the use of *predetermined* "standard" machine hour recovery rates, as have legions of textbooks since.

Church's "supplementary rates"

Instead of the modern practice of accounting for under or over recovery of overhead, Church recommended the use of

---

[3]Various absorption bases such as material value and labour hours have been recommended in addition to Church's machine hours. One of Johnson and Kaplan's criticisms of US practice in the 1980s was the excessive and uncritical use of labour-based overhead recovery despite the reducing importance of labour as a proportion of cost. J&K cite Church as an early advocate of "sophisticated" absorption costing: the forerunner of activity-based costing. However, Church's proposals, based on machine hour rates, seem entirely consistent with "conventional" absorption methods throughout the twentieth century.

"supplementary rates" which would lead to two costs of each order. He saw the "true cost" of the order as based on predetermined rates and the "apparent cost" after an addition based on the supplementary rates. In a forerunner of the "excess capacity" debate, Church argued that: "The latter cost is true cost *plus a percentage to represent a proportionate share of the wasted manufacturing capacity . . .*" [emphasis as original] (p. 74).

Although supplementary rates appear to have been little used, Church's reasons for recommending them provide insight into the practices of the time:

> First, it is a concession to those accountants who desire to get rid of all shop expense onto product as they have been accustomed; secondly, there is a certain amount of danger of establishing a precedent to the effect that departmental expense can be written off to Profit & Loss; thirdly, there is a distinct advantage in having the whole story told in respect to each order . . . (p. 74)

Church's ideas in practice

Johnson and Kaplan (1987), and Boyns (1998) refer to an application of Church's ideas by Hans Renold. This industrialist visited America, became familiar with the work of F. W. Taylor and Church and, returning to the UK, introduced the new costing method in his company at the turn of the century. His son, Charles Renold, later said that, when he entered the family business in 1905, Church's system "was in its first full flush of enthusiasm" (Renold, 1950: 113, quoted by Boyns). However, by 1910, it was realised that the system could not be kept up to date and the costs produced "gave no convenient guide to action". It seems that, despite their logic, Church's ideas were not easily applied and the results did not live up to their theoretical promise.

Spread of absorption costing: Uniform costing

There were, though, other forces that helped the spread of absorption costing. The "uniform costing" movement was traced by Solomons (1950a, b) from 1891 when the first system was developed by the National Association of Stove Manufacturers in the US, to 1947 when there were about 26 schemes in the UK and perhaps 150 schemes in the US. This did not mean that absorption

costing practice was either widespread or uniform but, as: "...
uniform costing schemes, as at present conceived, always aim at
computing average total cost..." (Solomons, 1950a: 249), there
can be little doubt that the uniform costing movement helped to
spread absorption costing methods.

In the UK, the earliest uniform costing scheme was introduced in
the printing industry and Mitchell and Walker (1997) analyse the
motives for this. In the late nineteenth century the printing industry became intensely competitive and, in 1901, printing employers
responded to heavy unionisation by establishing a national
employers' organisation, the British Federation of Master Printers
(BFMP). Costing methods employed in the industry were very
diverse and there was much criticism of "blind tendering" and
under-pricing. The BFMP saw the development of industry-wide
uniform costing as a key response to these problems and formally
approved a system of uniform costing in 1913.

The "... key components of the new system" are outlined by
Mitchell and Walker (see Figure 2.1).

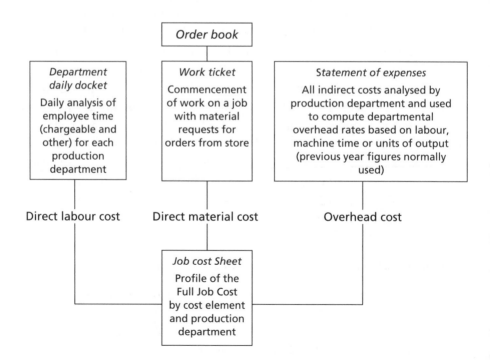

Figure 2.1 The BMPF system of uniform costing (Mitchell and Walker, 1997)

The BMPF system was consistent with the principles of factory accounting and of absorption costing and Mitchell and Walker note that the system: ". . . did not contain any particular technical novelty. Its key elements of cost recording and departmental overhead rates and the detailed analysis of over and under absorptions of production overhead were all well established techniques by the opening years of the twentieth century . . ." This observation is reinforced by Ahmed and Scapens (2000) who also note that the recommended procedures were not novel, quoting Church, 1901; Elbourne, 1914 and Hazell, 1921 as contemporary sources of theory.

Uniform costing had a long history and was still promulgated after the Second World War. Trade associations such as the Association of Bronze and Brass Founders, the British Iron and Steel Federation and the Federation of British Rubber and Allied Manufactures were publishing revised editions of their uniform costing systems in the late 1950s.[4] (These texts were reviewed by *The Cost Accountant* in March 1959 p. 362, May 1959 p. 436 and January 1960 p. 25, respectively.)

Spread of absorption costing: UK Government policy in wartime

Loft (1986, 1990) sees government policy in the First World War as a key impetus in the spread and institutionalisation of cost accounting and Kilvington (1974) even saw the ICMA as "a by-product of war". To combat wartime profiteering, the Government came to rely on cost-based pricing and, in 1916, the Defence of the Realm Act was amended. "In determining such a price regard need not be had to the market price, but shall be had to the cost of production of the

---

[4]The BFMP was still publishing tracts on costing in 1971. However, by this time, the costing debate had moved on with a review for *Management Accounting* (January 1972: p. 7) criticising the book for being: ". . . not so much a study of cost accountancy for printers as a description of a revised Federation costing system . . . The most serious lack of debate is over the initial strategic choice . . . Instead the book flatly chooses its strategy as full absorption costing and marginal costing is dismissed . . ." By the 1960s, marginal or direct costing had become a force to be reckoned with and the theoretical dominance of absorption costing had begun to wane.

output so requisitioned and to the rate of profit usually earned in respect to the output of such factory or workshop before the war." (Loft, 1986: 144). Costs in government factories were used to set prices paid to other manufacturers of the same products and, for government contracts, ". . . it became a normal practice for firms to prepare their cost estimates using full-costing and a routine task for government accountants to verify those estimates" (Ahmed and Scapens, 2000). The increasing involvement of accountants in costing practices set the scene for the founding of the Institute of Cost and Works Accountants in 1919 (Loft, 1990) and for the spread of (absorption) costing techniques in British industry after the First World War.

The Second World War reinforced the costing practices that had been developed and enforced during the First and one government report was described as: "little short of an official textbook on cost accounting" (*The Accountant*, 15 March 1941: 205). That this gave further impetus to absorption costing can be seen by its concentration on ascertainment of production overhead costs with these being divided into *shop oncost* and *general overheads*. The Price Control Act of 1941 gave the Board of Trade the power to "fix a maximum price for almost any manufactured article" and to "use its own methods in computing the cost of production" (*The Accountant*, 23 August 1941: 98). [References to *The Accountant* quoted by Ahmed and Scapens.]

The hegemony of absorption costing

In the first half of the twentieth century, the theory of absorption costing dominated cost accounting texts. A typical treatment is supplied by Carter (1938: 850–876) who saw: "The primary object . . . [as] to ascertain the prime cost and total cost of the articles . . ." He continues: ". . . it is clear that *all* the expenses of the business not directly charged to the cost accounts must in some way or other be apportioned in an equitable manner to the various orders executed" (p. 865). While the most suitable method of attributing works "oncost" to departments and products "has given rise to much controversy" Carter takes the aim of cost accounting, the derivation of the total cost of product, as self evident, the issue being not *whether* but *how* this should be done.

Johnson and Kaplan's "Financial Accounting Domination" theory of cost accounting

There is little in our reading of, primarily UK, cost accounting history to support the Johnson and Kaplan view (based on their reading of US history) that cost accounting quickly came to be dominated by financial accounting and audit requirements. The early theorists were not influenced by financial reporting in wanting *all* costs traced to product (while separately attributing manufacturing and non-manufacturing costs) and Carter took this aim as self-evident. In the UK, there was no obvious outside pressure on cost accounting practice and Bigg made it clear that, in his experience, financial accounting did not mandate the use of absorption costs (1950: 245):

> "It is often the practice for Balance Sheet purposes to value stocks of finished goods and work in progress at works cost or even prime cost . . . [However] . . . This practice is again merely the outcome of a financial policy . . . [and the Cost Accounts will] . . . represent the *real* cost of production" [emphasis as original].

This suggests, first, that the cost accounts being kept separately from the financial accounts should not be unduly influenced by the requirements of financial reporting and, second, that a variety of methods might be employed to value stock in the financial accounts. However, the "real" (fully absorbed) cost of production would be derived within the cost accounts.

Neither uniform costing nor the wartime uses of costing were driven by financial accounting pressure. Both Mitchell and Walker (1997), and Ahmed and Scapens (2000) conclude that uniform costing in the printing industry aimed to inflate prices to the mutual benefit of both employers and employees. Conversely, the government's motivation was in the use of absorption costs as a means of containing or reducing prices.

Neither does Solomons (1950b) provide any evidence that uniform costing was influenced by the requirements of financial reporting. He sets out the objectives of uniform costing. First, to improve knowledge of costs so as to improve pricing policy and reducing inefficiency and waste. Second, to eliminate competition due to imaginary cost differences. Third, to allow firms across the industry to benefit by pooling information. Fourth, to facilitate research into common problems such as which production methods were most efficient. There is no suggestion of financial accounting "interference" in these motives for the development and use of uniform (absorption) costing.

In the first half of the twentieth century the motivations for the development and use of absorption costing seem unrelated to financial regulation and UK writers did not anticipate "interference" by financial accounting in cost accounting practice.

Standard costing

There was a second major innovation in the early years of the twentieth century: the development of standard costing. "Scientific management" in the US set the scene with the development of standard times for the labour in each production process. And, for overhead, there was already a hint of standard costing in Church's recovery rates, to be based on normal (not actual) levels of expense and volume.

Solomons (1952) claims that the first complete standard costing system was introduced at the Boss Manufacturing Company in 1911 and the "standard costing movement" was spread by leading figures such as Harrington Emerson and G Charter Harrison. Harrison's (1930) book, *Standard Costs*, provides us not only with valuable insights into the development of standard costs but also with his contemporary view of existing systems which he refers to as "the job-order cost plans". These were the outcome of late nineteenth/early twentieth century debates: booking material and labour costs to jobs and absorbing manufacturing overhead so as to establish the actual cost of each job produced (see Figure 2.1). These procedures could become very complex (as at Renold).

Each "wave" of costing ideas has been "sold" by disparaging existing practices and Harrison saw "actual costing", based on the "job order cost plan", as a suitable target. He writes:

> At the 1928 National Convention of the National Association of Cost Accountants, G. R. Lohnes, Controller, National Cash Register Company, told about the job-order cost system introduced by his

company in Dayton a number of years ago. After the system had
been in operation over a year and was employing 100 clerks to
operate it, the late John H. Patterson, founder of the company and
then its president, made enquiry as to the cost of a particular
model of register. After some delay the cost department informed
him that due to the immense amount of detail work required in
the operation of the system, the cost data had not reached a stage
where they could furnish the cost of any complete register, but
they could furnish him any information he might want as to the
costs of individual parts. Any one who knew Mr. Patterson needs
not to be informed that this incident represented the end of the
cost department; the system and the clerks went out overnight.
(Harrison, 1930: 5)

Harrison (1930: 6–8) expands on the deficiencies of contemporary
job-order costing systems. After noting that systems could give reliable information as to actual labour and material costs of product
he goes on to say that this is often not the case for burden.[5] ". . . the
serious mistake was usually made of distributing to costs all of the
factory burden in the month regardless of the amount of production . . ." (It would seem that Church's predetermined rates were
not always adopted.) Harrison goes on to list further criticisms of
job-order cost plans. First, there was delay in furnishing information. Second, it was necessary to compare one batch with another
if inefficiencies in production were to be revealed. Third, the
enormous amount of detailed information generated was almost
unusable by factory management. And, fourth, such systems were
excessively costly.

This last point was a major plank of Harrison's argument in favour
of standard costing. He points out (pp. 12–13) that, if standard costs
were adopted, matters would be much simpler: "Under the standard cost plan . . . piecework and standard are the same. If the piece
rates are changed, the standard costs are changed. No cost accounting at all is required as regards piece-work operations." Thus,
according to Harrison, for piecework wages and materials issued as
specified, standard costs furnish management with the product cost
information required and exception reporting allows managers to

---

[5]Burden is the American equivalent of overhead.

concentrate on those areas where inefficiency has been revealed. Harrison reports (p. 5), that having assisted the National Cash Register Company in the introduction of standard costs, despite a great increase in variety, complexity and volume: ". . . entirely satisfactory results are obtained from a department totalling 20 employees as compared with the 100 formally employed."

Variances

Johnson and Kaplan (1987: 51) give credit for the first comprehensive exposition of variances to ". . . two management consultants, Harrington Emerson and G. Charter Harrison. Harrison followed Emerson and in 1918 became the first person to publish a set of equations for the analysis of cost variances." By 1930, the theory of variances had been extensively worked out and Harrison (1930: 49–72) devotes a chapter to setting out "Cost and Profit Variation Formulas" [Chapter Title]. His "wage rate variation" and "time variation" formulas are exactly equivalent to modern wage rate and efficiency variances and he then proceeds to a number of "complex cost formulas". These include "cost variations" due to: calendar variations, idle time, production efficiency, labor rate variations, labor time variations, material prices, material consumption, number of set-ups, time making set-ups, variations in distributive expenses, variations in miscellaneous expenses, variations in the rates of salary paid and variations in the salaried staff.

On the calculation of these variances it is difficult to resist the following quotation:

> The problem of making practical use of cost formulas has been solved by the development of a form of cost and variation analysis sheet (Figure 17), which renders it possible for these formulas to be used rapidly and correctly by ordinary office workers. This method proves the truth of Taylor's statement that some way can always be found of making practical, everyday use of complicated scientific data, which appear beyond the experience and range of the technical training of ordinary practical men. (Harrison, 1930: 61)

The reader will not be surprised to learn that "Figure 17" (see Figure 2.2) does not seem particularly simple.

COST AND VARIATION SHEET

Department: Press   Month of May 1928

FIGURE 17

No.	Account Name	Class	Actual at Actual — Quantity or Hours	A — Price or Rate	Amount	Actual at Standard — B — Price or Rate	Amount	Std. Staff B1 — Salaries	Monthly Standard Cost — C — For Stand. Month	D — Actual Month	E — For Hours Actually Worked by Dept.	Stand. Cost H — of Months Production	Net 1 — Increase or Decrease H-A	Variation in Fixed Charges due to Fluctuation in Production — 2 Calendar Idle Time	3	4 Production Efficiency	Labor 5 — Rates	6 — Time	Material 7 — Price	8 — Consump	Distrib. Exp. 9	Expense 10	Salaries 11 — Rates	12 — Staff
	Department Hours								212	218	200												
	Ratios							101.9179	192.192	195.192		200.00						B-A H-B 100.00 100.00						
	Producing Labor	p	5000	.52	2600.00	.50	2500.00	—	3000.00	—	—	2400.00	200.00											
	Foreman	b			225.00		200.00	—	200.00	—	—	65.00	65.00	D-C 5.66	E-D 16.98	H-F 28.66					B-A 25.00	C-B	
	Inspector	e	4.37 Weeks		194.16	4.200	186.00	—	200.00	—	—	145.92	46.08	D-B 1.65	E-D 15.49	H-F 26.17					B-A 8.96	B1-B	
	Annealer	d	220	.65	143.00	.65	143.00	—	137.80	130.00	—	110.24	32.76			H-E 19.76	B-A 13.00	E-B 13.00					—	
	Shop Clerk	d	200	.55	110.00	.50	100.00	—	100.00	—	100.00	84.40	25.20			H-E 15.20	B-A 10.00	E-B —						
	Truckers & Sweepers	d	600	.42	252.00	.40	240.00	—	150.00	160.00	135.68	716.32			H-E 24.32	B-A 12.00	E-B 10.00	B-A 6.00 H-B 2.00	B-A 5.00 H-B 15.00					
	Lubricants & Supplies	p			96.00		90.00	—	100.00	—	80.00	16.00												
	Misc. Maint. Supplies	p			80.00		75.00	—	75.00	—	60.00	20.00												
	General Factory Expense	f			190.00			—	141.67	—	113.34	76.66									H-A 76.66			
	Depreciation	b			100.00		100.00	—	180.00	180.00	135.62	176.00		D-C 22.08	E-D 66.23	H-F 111.85					C-A 20.00		
	Power	f			220.00			—	300.00	—	240.00	10.00							H-B 20.00					
	Floor Space	f			90.00			—	100.00	—	80.00	10.00							H-B 10.00					
	Tools	p			600.00			—	300.00	—	400.00	200.00									H-A 200.00			
	TOTAL				3600.88			—	5792.56	—	4634.05	1069.81												

* Indicates Red Figure Signifying Cost Increase

Figure 2.2   Cost and variation sheet (Harrison, 1930: 17)

Following the zeal of the early pioneers variance analysis has been somewhat simplified,[6] first by virtually ignoring non-manufacturing variances, and second, by concentrating attention on the most obvious manufacturing variances. Continuous "repackaging" of variance analysis has led to summaries such as that in Figure 2.3.

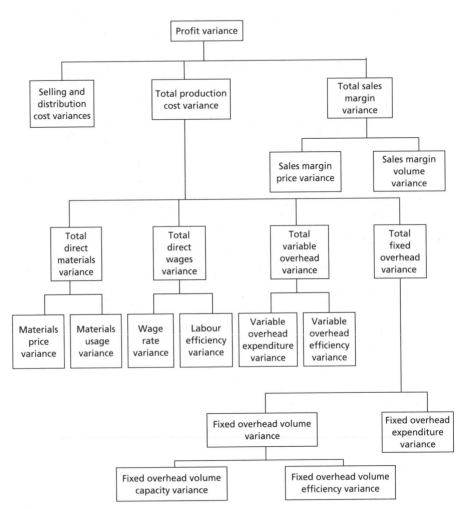

Figure 2.3 Chart of variances (adapted from Drury, 5th edition, p. 683) by kind permission of Thomson Learning

[6]Although, before its simplification, all the possible complexities were explored. Edis (1965) notes that "Bigger and better variance analysis seems to be the maxim of some accountants, and those in practice as consultants are often the biggest offenders." He goes on to question the need for calendar variances. But development continued with, for example, Middleton K. A (1968) developing 2-, 3- and 4-way overhead variances.

In the first quarter of the twentieth century there were significant advances in the theory of cost accounting with the development of factory accounts, absorption costing, standard costing and, also in this era, budgeting. For Johnson and Kaplan, the development of theory then stopped with only minor changes until the 1980s. However, we would argue that direct or marginal costing and its "battle" with absorption costing represented a major theoretical debate and, indeed, the literature of the time referred to "the direct costing controversy". We turn to this next.

The direct costing controversy

If Harrison had questioned the practicality of absorption costing methods based on the "job order cost plan", Harris (1936) asked a more fundamental question: "What did we earn last month?" (title). He concluded that absorption cost–based statements could not satisfactorily answer the question and coined a new term, "direct costing", for his preferred system (Armstrong, 1995).

Direct costing is a means of reporting historic results that contrasts with absorption costing because it leads inexorably to the valuation of inventory at variable, rather than full, manufacturing cost: "perhaps the most controversial issue of direct costing" (NACA, 1953: 1097). Direct costing statements do not yield the same value for profit as absorption-based statements when stocks are rising or falling and one of the key issues, as implied by Harris' paper, is which of these is more "correct".

Drury's (2000) diagrammatic summary of absorption and variable costing systems is shown in Figure 2.4. It may seem surprising that an apparently slight difference in the two systems could have given rise to such controversy. The only difference between absorption and variable costing is in the treatment of manufacturing fixed overhead, included in stock under absorption costing but written off to P&L as a period cost under variable costing. To understand the depth of the controversy we summarise below, it must be remembered that the theory of absorption costing had been under development for half a century and, for some cost accountants, it represented their claim to professional expertise. Variable costing threatened a thoroughgoing simplification that might adversely impact the cost accounting "professional project".

Absorption costing

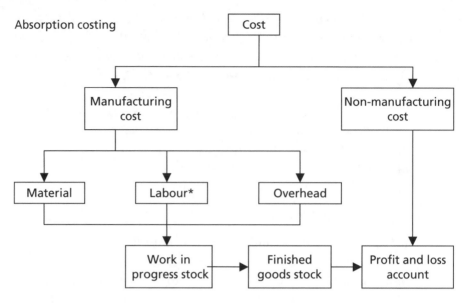

* It is assumed, here, that labour is a variable cost

Variable costing

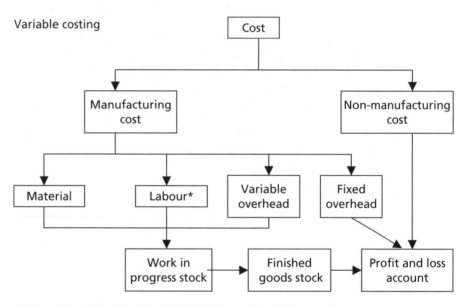

* It is assumed, here, that labour is a variable cost

Figure 2.4 Adapted from Drury 5th edition, p. 203, by kind permission of Thomson Learning

A note on terminology is useful here. "Direct costing" was the term coined by Harris and is often used in the US. However, in the UK, these systems have often been referred to as marginal costing systems. Unfortunately, neither term is literally accurate as the intent is to include all manufacturing variable costs in the value of stock, not just "direct costs" or the economists' "marginal costs". Drury tries to clarify the issue by referring to "variable costing systems". As an aside we note that this has the advantage of leaving the term "marginal costing" to refer to forward-looking techniques related to the use of relevant costs for decision making.[7]

The 1950s saw great interest in direct costing and the *National Association of Accountants* in the US held two conferences devoted exclusively to the subject. ". . . On each occasion registrations had to be limited . . . In total, approximately 800 persons attended the two conferences" (NAA, 1961: 1).

In the UK, the first paper to use the term "direct costing" was that published in *The Cost Accountant* by Reece in 1940 (Armstrong, 1995). There was swift reaction from a defender of the, now well established, absorption costing methods:

> Direct costs foster the old gross profit idea so strongly adhered to by auditors. . . . But it has been the Cost Accountant's hard won privilege to be able to point out how much of this margin is required to be absorbed in order to show a net profit. If that privilege is to go we must all start from scratch (Amsdon, 1941; quoted in Armstrong, 1995).

However, others adopted the new technique with enthusiasm and, as we have seen before (and will see again) consultants extolled the virtues of the new system while drawing attention to the deficiencies of the old. Two consultants, Lawrence and Humphreys (1947) set out the principles of the method in: ". . . the first book devoted to the subject of Marginal Costing" (1947: v). After referring to the problems of understanding absorption costing–based financial statements they suggest that: "Now, if the same account is presented on a Marginal basis, it becomes

---

[7]One could argue that "marginal costing" is not really an appropriate term for this group of techniques either. However, it seems better to use the term inappropriately once rather than twice.

alive. The Directors do not have to apologise for their lack of interest in the detailed account normally provided" (1947: 49). Lawrence and Humphreys claim to have introduced the technique: "in a sufficiently varied number of industries and business enterprises to give them the utmost confidence in its efficiency" (1947: vi) and they set out to explain what marginal costs are (i.e. variable costs) and to show the advantages of a marginal P&L account over its absorption cost counterpart. They see total costs as ". . . based on a misconception of the nature of overhead expenses. They are never correct . . . [and] (1) are incapable of being incorporated in clear statements of costs and profits; (2) slow down the production of periodic statements of cost and profit and loss" (p. 25).

Interest in direct costing built up in the UK during the 1950s and so did opposition to it. When the *Institute of Chartered Accountants in England and Wales* (ICAEW) journal *Accountancy* published "Direct costing – its pros and cons" (September 1955 p. 2) an anonymous reviewer for *The Cost Accountant* echoed Amsdon's earlier comments: "Are we to go back along the road we have so arduously travelled in reaching present normal practice?" (November 1955: 196)

But others were clear that direct costing was simpler and more meaningful. Thompson, a works manager, did not mince his words. He saw the apportionment or allocation of overheads as:

> pointless, wasteful and confusing . . . there can be no advantage in lumping them all together in the first place, and then breaking them down on some mysterious basis . . . The application of this practice to the preparation of control statements is bad enough because it is so pointless. When it is extended to the provision of information which is to be the basis for managerial decision it becomes, in most cases, positively dangerous. (1958: 15)

By the 1960s, accountants had the choice of absorption costing and direct (marginal or variable) costing. Either system could be combined with standard costing and they were free to choose any of these variants unhindered by external reporting constraints. However, although we can see little evidence of Johnson and Kaplan's "financial dominance" in pre-1960 UK costing history, financial regulation would eventually have its impact.

Stock valuation for external financial reporting

In 1960, the Council of the ICAEW issued its Recommendation on Accounting Principles No. 22: Treatment of Stock-in-Trade and Work in Progress in the Financial Accounts. This stated that non-manufacturing overhead should be written off as a period cost but, reflecting practice, several alternative treatments of manufacturing overhead were allowed. The Recommendation concluded that cost should include all expenditure directly incurred in bringing an item to its present location and condition "together with such part, *if any*, of the overhead expenditure as is appropriately carried forward" (ICAEW, 1960: 633, emphasis added). Matthews (1961: 52) welcomed "the complete absence of dogmatism" in Recommendation 22.

However, methods of stock valuation affect profit and hence tax liability and the Inland Revenue's hardening attitude on the issue can be seen by its persistence in the case of *Duple Motor Bodies* v. *Inland Revenue Commissioners*. Duple Motor Bodies had employed a system of direct costing for many years but this was challenged by the Inland Revenue. Eventually reaching the House of Lords, their lordships (again) ruled in favour of the company declaring that, since the accountancy profession could not agree on one method of costing (Recommendation 22 was about to be issued), they saw no reason why their lordships should (*Accountancy*, April 1961: 194).

That the Inland Revenue was unwilling to let the matter rest can be inferred from a letter from Sir Alexander Johnston (Chairman of the Board of Inland Revenue) to the President of the ICAEW. The letter stated that the Revenue would like to see overheads included in stock valuation. The vast majority of manufacturing concerns used the oncost method and the Revenue would not wish to see a mass switch to the direct method in the wake of the Duple case (*Accountancy*, May 1961: 311).

In the 1960s, financial reporting directives did not require that absorption costing methods be employed in the valuation of stock. However, there were indications that the Inland Revenue was exercising pressure on those companies that employed direct costing to cease the practice and on those that employed absorption costing to continue that practice.

Cost accounting debates: 1961–1975

Despite resistance from tax authorities, interest in direct costing continued to increase in the UK. In the mid-1960s, a report commissioned by the ICAEW extolled its virtues. Conventional (absorption costing) accounting statements, especially if combined with standard costing, were seen as complex and, for accountants, there was: "the danger of their [managers] being presented with too complicated a statement . . . [and] . . . not fully understanding it, they may in a short time tend to ignore it altogether" (Dixon, 1966: 76). In support of direct costing, Dixon echoed Lawrence and Humphreys: "It is theoretically incorrect, and inexpedient in practice, to carry forward fixed expense, applicable to one period in time, into a subsequent period of time in the valuation of stock" (p. 91).

By the mid-1960s, the debate had swung in favour of the new system and, by the 1970s, the superiority of direct costing for management information was largely taken for granted. Sizer's views reflect this shift. In the early 1960s, he had urged caution because "Marginal costing may be a dangerous technique in the hands of the uninitiated" (1963: 88). However, ten years later, he was clear that: "absorption costs may provide misleading information for decision making and lead to the calculation of overhead variances that are not understood by managers when a standard absorption costing system is employed" (Sizer, 1973: 50).

However, the Accounting Standards Steering Committee was constituted in 1970 and one of its first tasks was to review accounting for stock. *Statement of Standard Accounting Practice No. 9: Stocks and Work in Progress* (SSAP9) took effect in 1975 following some debate on its Exposure Draft predecessor (ED6) issued in 1972 and it enshrined, not direct costing, but the principles of absorption costing. ED6 noted that:

> No area of accounting has produced wider differences in practice than the computation of the amount at which stocks and work in progress are stated in the financial accounts. . . . [The statement's aim was to] narrow the differences and variations in those practices and to ensure adequate disclosure in the accounts. (Accounting Standards Steering Committee, 1972: 158)

Invoking the matching principle as its rationale, ED6 included a remarkably enduring statement:

> In order to match costs and revenue, "cost" of stocks and work in progress needs to include all expenditure which has been incurred in bringing the product or service to its present location and condition. Such costs will include all related overheads, even though these may accrue on a time basis. (Accounting Standards Steering Committee, 1972: 158)

Thus was the die cast for UK stock reporting in the next quarter century.

Cost accounting becomes "management accounting"

After the Second World War there was a distinct shift as discourse moved from "cost accounting" to "management accounting". In the UK this can be traced to the productivity report, *Management Accounting*, published by the Anglo-American Council on Productivity (1950). This report defined management accountancy as ". . . the presentation of accounting information in such a way as to assist management in the creation of policy and in the day-to-day operation of the undertaking" (viii). Following the introduction of "managerial accounting" in the US, and "management accounting" in the UK, textbooks had a new emphasis. Horngren (1962) links the old with the new in his title *Cost Accounting: A Managerial Emphasis* and announces (dust jacket) its emphasis on "different costs for different purposes".

The development of cost accounting had focused on the recording of historic costs in the ledger accounts and their attribution to jobs, batches, processes, contracts, etc. and, as we have seen, this had itself given rise to debate and controversy. There was, though, another debate that concerned itself with more general uses of cost information. As early as 1923 J. Maurice Clark published his book *The Economics of Overhead Costs* in which he set out his analysis of "different costs for different purposes" (Chapter IX, pp. 175–203). The relevant costing treatments he outlined for different circumstances – plant not yet built, plant operating but a change in method of production considered, price reduction as a means of increasing demand and so on – stand as testament to his depth of understanding. By the 1950s and 1960s textbooks could draw on Clark's ideas of relevant costs for decision-making and on the theories of management by exception that had evolved from the development of standard costing and budgeting.

Horngren (1962) reflected the spirit of the times as the "old" cost accounting gave way to a "new" managerial emphasis. The change is signalled by the arrangement of material: "The most interesting and important management topics appear early in the book" (dust jacket). The Preface sets these out as the role of the accountant, cost behavior, responsibility accounting, standard costs, flexible budgets, cost structures for control and motivation and relevant costs for special decisions. Cost accounting, now relegated in importance, becomes increasingly "packaged" for student consumption. Direct manufacturing costs are to be traced to products and factory overhead is to be allocated on ". . . some common denominator or base, such as expected total machine hours, direct labor hours or direct labor dollars for the ensuing year" (Horngren, 1962: 92). Absorption costing methods now compete for space not only with the "new" standard costing, responsibility accounting and decision-making ideas but also with direct costing.

In the UK Drury's (1984) text took the process of structuring and "packaging" *Management and Cost Accounting* [title] a step further. Now cost accounting is clearly separated from more managerially oriented techniques and is obviously part of financial reporting ("Part II: Cost Accumulation for Stock Valuation and Profit Measurement"). Other parts of Drury's text deal with "Information for Decision Making", "Information for Planning and Control" and "Divisional Performance Evaluation".

The impact of technology: The MRP "crusade"

In the decades following the Second World War, the theory of cost and management accounting matured into a rational and coherent whole. The management accountant could advise managers in key areas such as decision-making, planning, control and evaluation, supported by systems of cost collection and accumulation that underpinned financial reporting systems as well as the edifice of management accounting theory. And, from the 1960s, computers meant that these theories could be harnessed by increasingly powerful information technologies.

Johnson and Kaplan (1987) see the computerisation of existing cost systems as a "lost opportunity."[8] However, we think this view does little justice to the issues by overestimating the computing power available in the 1960s, underestimating the difficulties involved in developing new computer systems and ignoring the inter-relationships between cost and production systems.

Lilly (2001), an IBM employee from 1960 till 1968, describes the development of Materials Requirements Planning systems. These systems were (and are) based on "bills of material" for each product that specify which materials and components are required in each sub-assembly and which sub-assemblies are needed to build the finished product. In the early 1960s, IBM saw the bill of materials (BOM) processor idea as an ideal computer application, although Lilly felt that: "In truth, it was not meant to serve so much as system schematic as a blueprint for successfully marketing the System/360" (p. 25).

In 1968, when Lilly left IBM: "Other than the IBM PICS system – such as it was – and a program offered by Honeywell, there were no other packaged manufacturing systems in the market." However, MRP systems became increasingly prevalent in the 1970s with the American Production and Inventory Control Society (APICS), seeking funding and certified professional status for its members, launching "the APICS MRP crusade" of 1972 and 1973. Attendance at seminars was charged but the presenting consultants gave their services free and revenue was shared between the APICS local chapters and the national organisation.

The "MRP crusade" in the US was quickly reflected in the UK with MRP systems introduced in many UK manufacturing companies. In the 1970s and early 1980s these included Rockwell International, Westinghouse Brake & Signal Co. Ltd., 3Ms' Riker

---

[8]". . . and, most important, as great advances in information technology occurred, we would then expect managers to reconsider their decision not to invest in a more relevant and timely management accounting system. But by the time these events unfolded, the spirit and knowledge of management accounting systems design, developed and sustained throughout the hundred-year period 1825–1925, had disappeared. Organizations became fixated on the cost systems and reporting methods of the 1920s, starting in the mid-1960s, the system designers basically automated the manual systems they found in the factory" (Johnson and Kaplan, 1987: 14).

Laboratories, Hamworthy Hydraulics, Xerox, Lansing Bagnall Limited, Sperry New Holland, Molins, Marconi, Eaton Ltd and Leyland Trucks.[9] Early systems with evocative names such COBRA (Computerisation of Brake Areas), PROTOS (Production Oriented Terminal Operated System) and SOLAR (Supply Order Loading and Release) were largely developed in-house. However, in the early 1980s, greater use was made of proprietary systems such as IBM's MAPICS (Manufacturing, Accounting and Inventory Production Control System).

The emphasis, in virtually all the MRP case studies, is on production scheduling issues such as bills of material, stock records, "pegged" requirements, manufacturing capacity by "time bucket", etc. Costing is rarely mentioned, but is, nevertheless, integral to MRP systems. Chappell's (1978) exhaustive list of the uses of MRP at Hamworthy Hydraulics included: "Standard Costing . . . a relatively simple manipulation of the data base since all parent-component links, manufacturing methods and labour and overhead rates are known." Roxburgh (1983: 150) describes IBM's MAPICS, noting that the Product Data Management database: "can hold material, labour, and overhead costs at both standard and current values. It has a facility to roll-up costs level by level through the bill of material to produce product costs. It also has a 'what if' facility for simulating costs."

Mackison (1981), exceptionally, reported the use of MRP in product costing. His company, Conex-Sanbra, employed the IBM package, IPICS which: ". . . would give us most of what we wanted with the major problem being the costing module needed for Phase 2" (p. 131). He sets out the deficiencies from Conex-Sanbra's point of view: ". . . the costing module was a batch system, fixed overhead was not included as a separate cost element and most importantly . . . swarf recovery during the manufacturing process as a cost credit was ignored during the cost roll up" (p. 135). It seems that the IPICS software had provision for only a single overhead rate (per cost centre) and the standardised "cost roll-up" procedures could not cope with the particular costing issue of

---

[9]From the *Proceedings of the Annual Technical Conference of the British Production and Inventory Control Society*.

waste recovery at Conex-Sanbra. Mackison goes on to explain how these problems were overcome by customising the IBM package.

Burlingame (1979: 6) provides an insight into the inter-relationship between production and costing. "At one point during the implementation of the standard cost system, our controller came and asked me if I would delay making any engineering changes for a month or so to enable him to catch up with his standard cost." Burlingame felt that, in his company (Twin Disc Inc.), they had been fortunate in being allowed to implement manufacturing systems before financial ones. However, he knew that this was not always the case, quoting another experience where: "The annual engineering change rule quite obviously came from a standard cost system where the standards were set once a year . . ."

By the late 1970s, with the availability of proprietary MRP systems, Coneron (1978) was convinced that "M.R.P. if properly applied offers tremendous opportunities for improving customer service, operating efficiency, productivity . . .". However, installation of MRP systems was still not a task not to be underestimated. Hoolihan (1978), a consultant with Booz, Allen & Hamilton International, noted that "The Failure Rate of MRP Systems Has Been Phenomenal" and claimed that: "Improvement potentials of 25% are regularly identified . . . Yet these levels of improvement potential are being identified as many as ten years after the implementation of the computer-based management systems in the company." Even in the early 1980s Lee (1981) was surprised by "The high failure rate . . . since MRP is a thoroughly tested system."

All of this convinces us that the implementation of (standard) costing systems, based on the MRP systems of the 1970s was not simple. Both hardware and software technologies were relatively novel and these technologies imposed new disciplines and rigidities; inter-relationships between production and costing functions were redrawn; implementation could take many months or years and the systems might fail. In sum, we feel that the issues faced by the software designers and systems implementers of the 1970s go far beyond the automation "of the manual systems they found in the factory".

MRP implementations were still reported in the mid-1980s, for example, at Adams Foods (Crowcroft, 1985), Cyanamid of Greta

Britain Ltd. (Witham, 1985) and at Jafra Cosmetics International Ltd. (Graham and Harris, 1984). However, by now the focus of papers presented at BPICS conferences had moved away from MRP towards the use of micro computers, flexible manufacturing systems, JIT/kanbans, CAD/CAM, CIM and total quality. The "new manufacturing environment", heavily influenced by the success of Japanese companies using Just-in-time (JIT) and Total quality management (TQM), was shifting the production management agenda.

It was against the background of disillusionment with traditional MRP systems and considerable interest in new "Japanese" manufacturing systems that Kaplan (1985) undertook his early field studies and concluded that management accountants had missed the opportunities presented by computers by automating their existing, obsolete, systems. Our conclusion is different. The 1970s and early 1980s saw the development of integrated systems for stock control, order scheduling and material requirements planning and, as these systems included bills of material for each top-level product, it was natural to extend them to costing and stock and WIP accounting. Far from simply computerising the systems they found we believe that systems analysts designed computer systems in line with perceived "best practice". At that time, the conventional wisdom included standard costs for management control and absorption costing for financial reporting, all as set out in the neatly packaged presentations of leading academics.

Proprietary systems incorporating standard absorption costing were designed to be fully comprehensive, meeting the needs of auditors and financial reporting and providing the means of recovering manufacturing overhead costs by production cost centre. From a purely technical standpoint this was sensible because any company that wished to employ a direct or marginal standard costing system could simply ignore the overhead recovery facilities in the software.[10] However, the UK and the International stock

---

[10]Luscombe (1993) writing on the value of MRP systems, but post the "relevance lost" debate of the late 1980s, notes that: "Unfortunately MRPII is very good at reinforcing traditional management accounting practices. Standard cost roll-up procedures happily support the use of absorption costing, while labour reporting facilities allow detailed variance analysis to be performed" (p. 180). Luscombe goes on to note that these are not inescapable features of MRP systems, absorption rates for the recovery of fixed overhead do not *have* to be set.

accounting standards were published in the mid-1970s and pressures to conform would be intense. Combined with the increasing availability of computer systems, auditors' desire for accounting integration and, in multinationals, a desire for easy consolidation it is not surprising that many companies adopted computerised standard absorption costing systems. Whereas Johnson and Kaplan see the wave of computerisation as merely the automation of existing (long obsolete) systems, our analysis of UK costing history suggests that developments were a consequence of pressures that emerged in the 1970s. The interests of tax authorities, standard setters, auditors, software manufacturers and consultants combined to create the costing systems of the 1980s.

Our interpretation of UK cost accounting history sees companies implementing computerised costing systems during the 1970s and these were the systems that came under withering attack during the 1980s. These 1980s critiques are the subject of the next section.

2.3 Relevance lost and regained: Recent developments

The 1980s critique of cost and management accounting

As we mentioned, recent developments can hardly be understood without appreciating the impact of Johnson and Kaplan's (1987) "relevance lost" thesis of management accounting. Jones and Dugdale (2002) trace the origins of this attack on cost accounting's conventional wisdom to Harvard University in the early 1980s where a number of academics were concerned about the impact of global change on US manufacturing. Kaplan was appointed Professor of Accounting at Harvard in 1984, and soon (1985) reported his disappointment that a "select set" of innovative companies, despite embracing JIT, TQM and AMT, had failed to implement innovative accounting systems.

Nonetheless, concern that global manufacturing was changing while (management) accounting was failing to adapt, together with commitment to field studies, soon led to the "discovery" of ABC. First Cooper, with research assistants (Cooper, Weiss and Montgomery, 1985) reported their findings at the *Schrader Bellows Group* and then Kaplan, with research assistant, March, reported the case of

John Deere Component Works (March and Kaplan, 1987). Although referred to as "transaction based costing" at Schrader Bellows, at John Deere, the innovation was known as activity-based costing A third strand was added by Johnson's *Weyerhauser* case study (Johnson and Loewe, 1987). From this tripartite network, activity-based costing – with its three letter acronym, ABC – was subsequently marketed as a solution for manufacturing problems in the US (and for problems in other sectors and countries).

Another network, CAM-I, was also very concerned with finding solutions to perceived changes in global manufacturing. Brimson (1987) described CAM-I as a not-for-profit organization, formed in 1972, with large firm members based in the US, Europe and Japan. CAM-I had programs dealing with CAD and CAM and was concerned with the impact of cost accounting in automated environments. Within CAM-I there was a feeling that accounting systems were inhibiting advances in AMT, and financial reports were providing inadequate information.

As we have seen before, the prelude to new accounting systems is often an attack on the existing systems and this attack can be more focused if the "new" and "better" system has already been developed. By the mid–late 1980s Kaplan, Cooper and Johnson had a clear understanding of activity-based ideas and Brimson also understood these together with the potential of JIT and TQM to transform manufacturing.

Absorption costing "inaccurate"

Kaplan (1987) used the Schrader Bellows case to great effect in his efforts to discredit typical (computerised) absorption costing systems. The summary of "overhead per unit" for each of seven different valves (see Table 2.1) shows how much the "cost" of each product might vary in switching from the "old" absorption system to the "new" transaction-based system.

With figures like these to support his argument, Kaplan was able to claim that: "Product #10400, the product reported by the old cost system as having the highest margin, is in fact the biggest loser. When this company got an order for that product they should have shipped a ten dollar bill to the customer and said 'Thanks for the order; buy it from someone else.' "

Table 2.1: Kaplan (1987). Reproduced by kind permission of American Accounting Association (Mitchell and Walker, 1997, p. 92)

		Overhead per unit Cost per unit			Gross margin (rates)		
Product	Volume	Old	New	Dif. (%)	Old	New	Dif. (%)
10 000	43 562	$5.44	$4.76	−13	41	46	12
10 200	500	6.15	12.86	109	30	−24	−180
10 400	53	7.30	77.64	964	47	−258	−649
10 600	2 079	8.88	19.76	123	26	−32	−223
10 900	5 670	7.58	15.17	100	39	2	−95
11 200	11 196	5.34	5.26	−1	41	41	0
11 600	423	5.92	4.39	−26	31	43	39

Thus one attack on existing systems concerned the accuracy of overhead allocation. ABC promised a better method of tracing overhead to product and hence better information for decision-making. With overhead becoming an increasing proportion of total cost, Johnson and Kaplan (1987) were clear that the costing systems of the 1980s had become obsolete.[11] A better method was needed to fulfil "the most important goal for a product cost system . . . to estimate the long-run costs of producing each product, each saleable output, in the company's product line" (p. 234).

Cost accounting performance measures misleading

Simultaneously, Brimson (1987) was able to mount a wide-ranging attack on "traditional" performance measures derived from conventional standard costing, budgeting and variance analysis (see

---

[11]"Perhaps twenty years ago, when Management Information Systems (MIS) personnel or computer types first wandered into the factory . . . they automated, with few changes, the manual or electro-mechanical cost system they found there. . . . [But] the 1950 vintage systems . . . incorporated many simplifying assumptions . . . virtually all companies allocated cost center costs to products based on direct labor . . . Typically this fully burdened cost center labor rate was at least four times the actual direct labor rate paid to the workers. In some highly automated cost centers, it was not unusual for the rate to be ten or even fifteen or twenty times the hourly rate" (Johnson and Kaplan, 1987: 183–184).

Figure 2.5). Brimson's analysis was informed by his understanding of activity-based analysis (references to cost centres, overhead and activities), JIT production (references to delivery and excess inventories) and TQM (references to scrap and standard costs).

Measurement	Action	Result
Purchase price	Purchasing increases order quantity to get lower price. Ignores quality and delivery.	Excess inventory. Increased carrying cost. Supplier with best quality and delivery is overlooked.
Machine utilization	Supervisor runs machine in excess of daily unit requirement to maximum machine utilization.	Excess inventory. Wrong inventory.
Scrap factor built into a standard cost	Supervisor takes no action if no variance.	Inflated standard. Scrap threshold built in.
Standard cost overhead absorption WIP	Supervisor overproduces to get overhead absorption in excess of his expenses.	Excess inventory.
Indirect/direct head count ratio	Management controls the ratio not the total cost. Total cost not in control.	Indirect labor standards wrongly established.
Scrap $	Scrap $ drives corrective action priority.	Defect level impact on flow hidden in $.
Cost center reporting	Management focus is on cost centers instead of activities.	Missed cost reduction opportunities because common activities among cost centers are overlooked.
Labor reporting	Management focus is on direct labor, which is fixed and relatively small. Overhead which is large is overlooked.	Missed cost reduction opportunities. Major overhead activities not exposed.
Earned labor $	Supervisor maximizes earned labor. Keeps workers busy.	Excess inventory. Scheduled attainment given lower priority. Output is emphasized.
Overhead rate	Management controls the rate not the total cost.	Overhead levels improperly established. High cost activities hidden.

Figure 2.5 Brimson (1987). Reproduced by kind permission of the American Accounting Association

Costing developments in the 1980s and 1990s

With a powerful critique of existing absorption costing systems (inaccurate, encouraging production of excess inventory and "hiding" overhead by the use of increasingly inappropriate labour-based recovery rates) and standard costing (overemphasis on price at the expense of quality and delivery), existing theory had once again been destabilised.

Although involved in the early development of ABC, Johnson quickly had second thoughts about the utility of the technique: "As someone who helped put the activity-based concept in motion, I feel compelled to warn people that I believe it has gone too far. It should be redirected and slowed down if not stopped altogether" (Johnson, 1992: 26). The theory of ABC was, therefore, largely worked out by Kaplan and Cooper: Cooper and Kaplan (1988a, b, 1991, 1992), Cooper (1988a, b, 1989a, b), Kaplan (1988).

Early ABC was an attempt to improve the accuracy of the product costs generated by the computerised absorption costing systems of the 1980s. At John Deere a new Division Manager described the response to ABC: "Few things have generated more excitement. Even though it's still an allocation, it's such an improvement. Parts we suspected we were undercosting have turned out to be even more expensive than we thought" (March and Kaplan, 1987). The heart of ABC is to use many more "cost drivers" to attribute overhead to products and to recognise that many of these drivers vary not with product volume but with number of batches, sales orders, customers, etc. This increased sophistication could be expected to improve the allocation of overhead and, at John Deere, the results were intuitively sensible.

It would not be unreasonable to see early ABC as an improved version of absorption costing and Drury's presentation (Figure 2.6) depicts the technique in this light.

Renewed battles: Activity-based costing versus throughput accounting

The late 1980s claim that ABC provided a basis for deriving "correct" (fully absorbed) product costs provoked an entirely predictable response from the latter day supporters of direct or

(a) Traditional product costing system

Stage 1: Overheads assigned to production departments

Stage 2: Overheads allocated to products

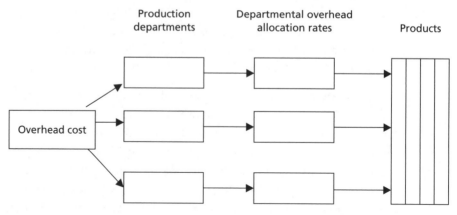

(b) Activity-based product costing system

Stage 1: Overheads assigned to cost centres/cost pools

Stage 2: Overheads assigned to products using cost driver rates

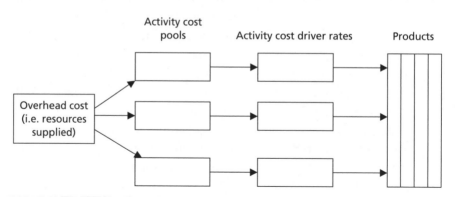

Figure 2.6 Comparison of traditional (a) and activity-based (b) costing systems (Adapted from Innes and Mitchell (1990)), Drury (1996: 299) by kind permission of Thomson Learning

marginal costing. Goldratt (with the assistance of a professional writer) authored *The Goal* (Goldratt and Cox, 1984), a book that sought to show how bottleneck management in manufacturing could significantly improve results. Goldratt's experience was shaped by his involvement in developing scheduling systems that improved on conventional MRP by taking account of the finite capacities of production facilities. This led him to recommend that bottlenecks should first be scheduled and all other (non-bottleneck) facilities should be subordinated to supplying these. This approach, later developed as the "theory of constraints" (TOC), saw overproduction on non-bottleneck machines as the creation of unwanted stock that would lead to longer delivery lead-times and an unresponsive facility.

In arguing that stock buffers were needed only to ensure that bottlenecks never ran out of work and other stocks should be minimised, Goldratt found that "Cost accounting is number 1 enemy of productivity" – because efficiency measures and over-head absorption encouraged stock building. Some of his criticisms therefore echoed those of Brimson. However, in addition, he favoured a form of variable costing that became known as "throughput accounting". Taking the view that, in modern facto-ries, most expenses, including labour costs, were fixed in nature, Goldratt concluded that profit would be maximised if "through-put", defined as sales less materials and bought out services, was maximised. Companies adopting his ideas tended to adopt vari-able costing systems, limiting the definition of variable costs to materials and bought out services.

It is possible that Goldratt (a physicist by training) might not recognise himself as the champion of variable costing. However, accountants who took an interest in his ideas quickly labelled throughput costing "super-variable costing" (Horngren *et al.*, 1996: 308) and Noreen *et al.* (1995: 13) felt that: "At the concep-tual level, throughput is indistinguishable from contribution mar-gin." The emergence of throughput accounting as a system of internal financial reporting raised once again the old issues con-cerning the valuation of stock and Smith (2000: 107) explained how companies could "bridge between throughput and GAAP financial statements" (chapter title).

Goldratt saw traditional absorption product costs as leading to inferior decisions and encouraging the building of unwanted stock. However, his reasons for criticising conventional absorp-tion costs were not the same as those of Kaplan and Cooper. Goldratt concluded that, as most costs in modern manufacturing are fixed, more emphasis should be placed on "throughput" and he therefore continued the traditions of direct, marginal or variable costing.

Kaplan, however, observing that overhead costs had grown rapidly in modern manufacturing plants, concluded that these costs were not fixed but variable. This led him to the view that "The only way to make this more visible is to get all the costs back to products. They are almost all variable" (Kaplan, 1987: 7.27). Kaplan's position was reminiscent of the early absorption costers: almost all costs should be traced to product. There were just two exceptions, excess capacity costs, which should be treated as period costs, and research and development costs for new products. In his implicit advocacy of "predetermined" recovery rates Kaplan continued a long tradition of absorption costing theory that stretched back to Church's "scientific machine hour rates". The difference between conventional absorption costs and activity-based costs was in the number of "cost pools" and the variety of "cost drivers" now identified as causing overhead costs.

Thus the battle lines were drawn again and the confrontation between absorption costing (ABC) and variable costing (throughput accounting) was played out in a series of three conferences sponsored by the (US) Institute of Management Accountants in the period 1988–1991.[12] Goldratt no doubt saw absorption costing as pointless and therefore doing it "better" as even more pointless: "Yes, the allocation can be done in this [activity-based] way. But for what purpose? Anyhow, we cannot aggregate them at the unit level, or even at the product level. So why play all these number games?" (Goldratt, 1990: 40).

His debates with Goldratt made a considerable impact on Kaplan, for, several years later he commented: "Recall the familiar expression that nothing focuses the mind so much as an imminent hanging. Well running a close second place is engaging in public debate with Goldratt who is an articulate and persuasive advocate of his deductive theory of constraints" (Kaplan, 1998: 107). A period of reflection led to dramatic transformation in the (theoretical) nature of ABC.

---

[12]Formerly *National Association of Accountants.*

Activity-based costing reformulated

The reformulation of ABC meant that it became a technique for predicting resources *used* rather than a method of allocating resources *supplied*. And, when this development was allied with a unit-batch-product-facility cost hierarchy ABC underwent a strange metamorphosis.

The transition from "first wave" (better absorption costing) ABC to "second wave" (better marginal costing) ABC is traced by Jones and Dugdale (2002). Cooper and Kaplan (1991) distanced themselves from (their) "first wave" ABC commenting that: "Initially, managers viewed the ABC approach as a more accurate way of calculating product costs." Then they went on to expound a revised version of ABC that no longer held out the promise of better or more accurate unit costs:

> *ABC is a powerful tool – but only if managers resist the instinct to view expenses at the unit level* . . . Managers must refrain from allocating all expenses to individual units and instead separate the expenses and match them to the level of activity that consumes resources. (Cooper and Kaplan, 1991, p. 130, italics indicate headline as original)

This approach is consistent with Cooper's (1990) ABC "cost hierarchy" that orders costs into "unit", "batch", "product-sustaining" and "facility-sustaining" levels and Kaplan now saw ABC as:

> The new approach to *contribution margin analysis* [which] derives from activity-based costing (ABC) . . . The ABC analysis strives to assign operating expenses to factors that cause them. Contribution margins can be calculated at the unit level; or after covering batch related expenses, and even after covering product line, customer, and distribution channel expenses. (quoted in Robinson, 1990, p. 5)

Thus "first wave" ABC was held out as a better form of absorption costing but ran into confrontation with the modern defenders of variable costing in the guise of "throughput accounting". Then ABC metamorphosed into its "second wave" now as a superior form of "contribution margin analysis". And it might be concluded that (once again) the proponents of direct/marginal/throughput costing were winning the theoretical battles.

However, if Kaplan had defected to the marginal costing camp, others were prepared to take up the challenge and Shank argued that marginal costing is: ". . . past its prime and it ought to be gotten rid of . . ." (quoted in Robinson, 1990: 16). And, despite the authors' re-designation of ABC as a better method of contribution analysis this was not universally accepted. Those who had been persuaded of the efficacy of first wave ABC were not necessarily persuaded by its contribution margin successor. Once ideas have been put into circulation they cannot be withdrawn so both strands of ABC thinking continue to circulate, co-existing uneasily together.

Integration of 1990s theory and technology

At the end of the twentieth century there were plenty of costing options available and examples can be found of companies employing throughput accounting, direct costing, contribution analysis, both first and second wave versions of ABC and, of course, "traditional" absorption costing. While there is a great diversity of practice we note that virtually all accounting applications now depend on computer systems and, often, proprietary software.

The software industry had matured since the "wild times" of the late 1960s and early 1970s when "A lot of 'smoke and mirrors' was sold as software" (Lilly, 2001: 37). In the early 1990s a new generation of software known as ERP (Enterprise Requirements Planning) made its appearance and new degrees of sophistication were achieved. Just as earlier software incorporated what appeared to be "best practice" costing systems in the 1970s, ERP software incorporated the theoretical developments of the 1980s and 1990s. Thus the market leading SAP product allows the user to employ either first or second wave versions of ABC as well as traditional absorption or direct costing systems. Figure 2.7 illustrates the manner in which ABC can be employed in "top-down" (absorption costing) mode or "bottom-up" (marginal costing) mode.

In the twenty-first century, practitioners have access to what could appear to be a bewildering array of techniques. Although the consultants who have "sold" new techniques have always claimed them as significant advances over the "old", "traditional" methods,

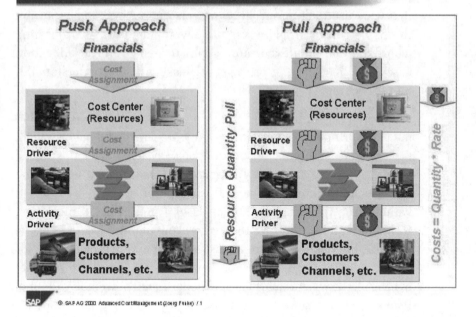

Push Approach

Financials

Cost Assignment

Cost Center (Resources)

Resource Driver   Cost Assignment

Activity Driver   Cost Assignment

Products, Customers Channels, etc.

Pull Approach

Financials

Cost Center (Resources)

Resource Driver

Activity Driver

Products, Customers Channels, etc.

Resource Quantity Pull

Costs = Quantity * Rate

SAP   © SAP AG 2000 Advanced Cost Management (Joerg Funke) / 1   47

Figure 2.7 Activity-based costing: Push versus pull SAP AG 2000, Reproduced by kind permission of Joerg Funke

it seems that accounting theories and techniques are reluctant to die gracefully. And the power of modern information technology and software packages means that virtually all the techniques developed in the twentieth century can now be made available, often in a single accounting package, itself integrated with other functional packages. Given these extensive possibilities what have manufacturing companies actually been doing? This is the subject of the next section.

2.4 Cost accounting practice in the 1990s

Introduction

Johnson and Kaplan (1987) with their "Relevance Lost" thesis attacked traditional (US) management accounting practice claiming that it was dominated by the requirements of financial reporting. A key element of the Johnson and Kaplan analysis was the hegemony of full absorption costing for stock valuation, a require-ment of US GAAP that had led to oversimplified full product costs that were used inappropriately in decision making. Their solution to this perceived problem was the development of ABC, a costing technique that employed more sophisticated overhead allocation bases and held out the prospect (at least in its early versions) of more "accurate" product costs.

The implicit assumption in Johnson and Kaplan's thesis was that manufacturing companies employed what Drury and Tayles (2000: 9) termed "traditional absorption cost systems". Such systems would, typically, integrate financial and management accounting systems and employ (standard) absorption costing in order to value stock. Johnson and Kaplan (1987) present a "Typical Cost System" (sub-heading, p. 184) where the standard cost of valve 60073 is broken down into material, labour and overhead costs for each operation (drill, face, tap, degrease, etc.). There are separate overhead recovery rates for each department (Assembly, Plating, Packing, etc.). Figure 2.8 is adapted from Johnson and Kaplan's text in order to show how an absorption cost is built up.

In Johnson and Kaplan's example the overhead recovery rates for Assembly, Automatic manufacturing, Plating, Packing and General machining are $24.21, 67.65, 84.16, 40.51 and 40.07 per labour hour respectively. Although several rates are used they are all based on labour hours; other bases such as material value and machine hours are not employed. Johnson and Kaplan argue that labour bases were becoming increasingly inappropriate as manufacturing became less

Standard cost report for part. . . .

	Material cost	Labor cost	Overhead cost	Total cost
Purchased part	$9.999			$9.999
Operation				
Drill		$0.555	$2.222	$2.777
Degrease		0.055	0.222	0.277
Total	9.999	0.610	2.444	13.053

Figure 2.8 Adapted from Johnson and Kaplan (1987: 185) by kind permission of Harvard Business School Publishing

and less labour intensive. And, in general, recovery bases that act as surrogates for product volume are insufficient because, increasingly, overhead is related to many transaction-based "cost drivers" such as the number of orders, setups, batches, material movements, etc.

Johnson and Kaplan's analysis was based on their observations in a limited number of US manufacturing concerns and some writers (Anthony, 1989: 18; Holzer and Norreklit, 1991: 7) felt that there was little information as to the state of actual cost and management accounting practice. Nevertheless, Kaplan and his collaborators (especially Cooper) were able to find a number of manufacturing companies that employed "traditional" absorption costing systems, typically based on standard costing techniques. For example, the Paramount Cycle Company (Sandretto, 1979) introduced standard costing in 1977/1978. Bridgeton Industries (Bost and Cooper, 1990) applied overhead to products via a single overhead pool using a rate of 435% of direct labour dollars in 1986/1987. "Institutional Furniture" (DeCoster, 1988) introduced standard costing in 19X3 [probably 1983 but reported as 19X3] and applied overhead to Work-in-Process at 154% of labour cost. Ingersoll Milling Machine Company allocated overhead to parts based on 14 overhead pools, all allocated on "direct labour dollars" with the exception of a single pool based on material cost. Many other examples could be cited including Seligram Inc., Digital Communications Inc., Mayers Tap, Fisher Technologies and, of course the two celebrated cases that saw the origins of ABC, Schrader Bellows and John Deere Component Works. Kaplan's evidence might have been anecdotal but it was broadly based in manufacturing industry and the cases were set out in sufficient depth to convince the reader that standard absorption costing systems were employed.

The corollary to the use of absorption costs for stock valuation is a P&L account that shows cost of sales at full absorption cost:

	£'000
Sales	xxxxx
Cost of sales	(xxxx)
Gross margin	xxxx
Non-manufacturing expenses	(xxxx)
Net profit	xxx

In this format, cost of sales is comprised of *manufacturing* costs and these are charged to P&L account as goods are sold. *Non-manufacturing* costs are written off to P&L account as they are incurred (period by period). By the 1980s, when Kaplan was carrying out his fieldwork, it seemed that many manufacturing companies were employing standard costing systems so that stock (and cost of sales) were valued at standard cost and manufacturing variances from standard were written off to P&L account.

Survey results

One of the consequences of the "Relevance Lost" furore was research in the early 1990s that aimed to identify the costing methods actually used in manufacturing industry. Drury and Tayles (2000: 21–22) reported that "With the exception of Finland and Norway, research relating to the usage of different costing methods tends to show that absorption costing dominates." They quoted Drury *et al.* (1993), Coates and Longden (1989) and Hendricks (1988) as evidencing the extent of full costing in the UK and the US, and Ask and Ax (1992) as indicating the domination of full costing in Sweden.

The most thorough survey of management accounting practice in UK manufacturing was that by Drury *et al.* (1993). They confirmed the prevalence of absorption costing in manufacturing industry because only 18% of respondents "never" or "rarely" used full costs (p. 8) and at least 95% indicated the use of one or more overhead recovery rates (p. 15). Additionally, 75% of respondents indicated that overhead recovery rates were used in tracing fixed manufacturing overheads to products in order to meet the requirements of SSAP 9 for external reporting (p. 17). However, the total dominance of absorption costing should not be assumed because there was a significant minority of respondents (20%) indicating that "Only variable costs are traced to products and the total amount of fixed overhead incurred during the period is apportioned between inventory and cost of goods sold" (p. 17). Also, although 58% "often" or "always" used total manufacturing or total cost in decision-making, 62% "often" or "always" used variable manufacturing cost or total variable cost. Thus, although absorption costing appeared to dominate, careful reading of Drury *et al.*'s results reveals continuing interest in variable costing, albeit by a minority of respondents.

In relation to standard costing, Drury and Tayles' study provided straightforward results with a significant majority of respondents (76%) reporting that they did employ standard costs (p. 38). Thus Drury and Tayles showed that (standard) absorption costing systems were prevalent although a significant minority of companies might employ variable costing systems and, for decision-making, many companies employed flexible approaches, combining both "full" and variable costs as appropriate.

Empirical research has therefore tended to support Johnson and Kaplan's position. Absorption costing appears to have been prevalent if not dominant for stock valuation across the US, UK and parts of Europe and there is evidence for the use of these "full" costs in decision-making. Berry *et al.* (2000) reported continuation of the status quo; in a limited sample of companies they found the ". . . use of standard costing was much wider than we had expected" and they went on to note that marginal and variable costs were little used.

If absorption costing practices were prevalent in the 1980s and early 1990s, *and* they were misleading, then one might expect considerable interest in and take-up of the proposed "solution": ABC. Bright *et al.* (1992) did indicate that, probably the majority, of UK companies were adopting or considering the adoption of "advanced" techniques such as ABC. However, by the mid – late 1990s it seems that take-up of ABC had stabilised at a relatively low level with Innes and Mitchell (1995a) and Innes *et al.* (2000) reporting approximately 20% of respondents adopting activity-based methods in both surveys.

Of course, ABC was not the only "solution" on offer. In a field study of companies that had adopted Goldratt's ideas, Noreen *et al.* (1995) reported (p. xxiv) that: "Instead of absorption costing, most of the TOC companies use a variation of variable costing in which it is assumed that direct materials are the only variable cost." Thus, despite the findings of Berry *et al.* reported above, Goldratt's ideas have had some impact on practice. And there is evidence of variable costing in a recent survey by Drury and Tayles (2000: 50) who reported that 50% of their respondents treated revenues less variable or direct costs (contribution) as their most important profitability measure.

Despite the indications of interest in activity-based and variable costing there appeared to be continuing use of "traditional" (stand-ard) absorption costing systems. The question of "lost relevance" resulting from "financial accounting domination" therefore remained unresolved. Drury *et al.* (1993) provided continuing support for the "relevance lost" thesis in gaining: "A general impression . . . that the methods employed for product costing and management control are influenced by the rules and proce-dures established for external financial reporting" (Executive Summary). However, Joseph *et al.* (1996: 90), based on a postal survey of UK management accountants found ". . . little evidence of a generally held belief that external reporting dominates inter-nal accounting." This was consistent with Hopper *et al.*'s (1992: 310) prior pilot study which found "no clear evidence of external reporting conventions or accounting standards being cited as adversely affecting management accounting systems".

Joseph *et al.*'s study was part of a larger CIMA sponsored project that included not only the questionnaire survey reported by Joseph *et al.* but also three longitudinal case studies and a field survey based on interviews with 15 of the accountants who had completed the postal questionnaire. Scapens *et al.* (1996) reported the results of this study. They found: ". . . no evidence of a direct impact of external reporting on day-to-day business decisions [although] . . . there still exists a framework of accountability which managers refer to" (p. ix). Additionally, and of relevance to this project, they still found: ". . . a strong tradition of budgeting and standard costing in the interviewees' organisations . . . [but] . . . there had been a lessening of the importance attached to variance analysis" (p. 145).

It is difficult to form a clear view as to whether financial account-ing does dominate internal accounting systems from the conflict-ing evidence on offer. In their most recent survey, Drury and Tayles (2000: 23) were more equivocal than before and, following Scapens *et al.* (1996) they note that a single database could be analysed to meet different needs. However, their evidence also suggests that, because manufacturing companies might employ unsophisticated or inflexible systems, "the claim that financial accounting dominates management accounting cannot be rejected."

No doubt influenced by a decade of theoretical debate and development there is now evidence of a changing role for management accountants with more emphasis on strategic management accounting and the management accounting interface within UK organisations. Friedman and Lyne (1997) provide evidence of the changes taking place. As a consequence of fieldwork in which they investigated companies that had taken up activity-based techniques they discerned a trend towards more proactive management accounting and proclaimed "the death of the bean counter". Similarly, Ahrens (1997), in a study of the relative roles of management accountants in the UK and Germany (based on studies in the brewing industry), found that, in contrast to their German counterparts, UK management accountants were now heavily involved as proactive members of management teams.

At the end of the twentieth century, management accountants had available to them an unprecedented array of theoretical techniques and the information technologies to use them. Additionally, they were increasingly seen as "business analysts", "lynchpins" and "facilitators" (Brignall *et al.*, 1999). Yet there was still evidence of the full absorption costing systems that had driven the charge of "relevance lost" in the 1980s. One of the authors of this book, familiar with standard absorption costing systems from his work in manufacturing in the 1980s, expected to encounter them when industrial visits were made as part of a research project to study pricing practices. However, the companies visited tended to use, not the gross profit style P&Ls that were expected, but variations of contribution style financial presentations. This stimulated the research project reported here. With some scepticism as to whether questionnaire survey style research would uncover the financial reporting and costing methods used in manufacturing companies a different methodology was adopted. The approach used, based on the systematic collection of documentary evidence and interviews, is described in the next section.

Methodology

3.1 Origins of the project

The *CIMA Contemporary Practices in UK Manufacturing Accounting* project emerged from an earlier study that was intended to investigate price setting in manufacturing industry and the relationship between marketers and accountants in the pricing setting process. This gained internal funding in 2000 from the University of the West of England for an exploratory survey.[13] Six companies were visited in the Spring of 2001, and both accountants and marketers were interviewed in each company. There were some interesting insights from these investigations, but we found no major issues in the relationship between accounting and marketing that excited our immediate attention. At the same time CIMA published a major research project that had addressed issues of marketing and accounting (Roslender and Hart, 2001). At this point the research team were beginning to lose interest in the project.

In the course of our interviews, however, we asked our interviewees how internal results were reported – with a view to then following up with questions about how this information might be used in pricing decisions. This investigation surprised one of the researchers. Having been employed in manufacturing industry in the 1980s where he had been exposed to standard absorption costing systems of the kind described in the literature review, he expected to find these in manufacturing companies at the beginning of the twenty-first century. Instead, a number of the companies were using quite different forms of internal reporting. This unexpected finding seemed far more interesting, and fundamental, than the issues uncovered around the accounting–marketing relationship.

In some ways the original project might be seen as a "failure" since the original aim to study the relationship between accounting and marketing had not been achieved. However, the University Research Committee was willing to accept that research is an unpredictable activity and hence its direction may well change during the course of the conduct of study. Indeed, it may well be argued that if studies did not throw up unexpected findings and

---

[13]The research team was David Dugdale (School of Accounting), Colwyn Jones (School of Sociology), Clive Nancarrow (School of Marketing) and Richard Collett (research assistant).

directions then they might not deserve the title "research".[14] The original studies led to a reformulation of the research project to focus specifically upon internal reporting practices. Four of the original companies agreed to assist us in pursuing this study and they became the initial pilot companies for a proposal to CIMA to explore innovation in manufacturing accounting. The grant for this was awarded in early 2002 and the current team began the study.

3.2 The initial pilot companies

In the original study the first company visited, Fuchsia Fabrics, operated a contribution style reporting system with an operating statement that could be summarised as in Table 3.1. This reporting

Table 3.1: Internal reporting format adopted at Fuchsia Fabrics			
	Consumer	Industrial	Linings
Sales	X	X	X
Less Materials[a]	(X)	(X)	(X)
Labour[b]	(X)	(X)	(X)
Power/water	(X)	(X)	(X)
Variable selling (transport)	(X)	(X)	(X)
Less Specific conversion overhead[c]	(X)		
Contribution	X	X	X
Less Sales and marketing overhead[d]	(X)	(X)	(X)
SBU contribution to shared overhead	X	X	X
Less Works overhead[e]	(X)		
Gross margin	X	X	X
Less Selling and admin	(X)	(X)	(X)
Net Margin	X	X	X

[a] At standard set at the beginning of each year.

[b] At standard based on full time regular employees.

[c] Works overhead related to conversion applicable only to the consumer business unit.

[d] There are separate sales and marketing operations for each business unit.

[e] Based on a machine hour recovery rate.

---

[14]Fellow researchers will no doubt note with some irony that not all grant providing agencies take such a relaxed view of research processes and outcomes, and researchers can sometimes find themselves constrained into delivering the promised outcomes even where they no longer regard these of any great significance and that an alternative discussion would be of more value.

format was obviously based on contribution principles with considerable trouble taken to identify variable overhead (power, water, selling expenses) and the attribution of particular overhead to a specific business unit (i.e. to Consumer Products) where this made sense. The format was surprising because the researchers had not expected to see almost a "textbook" standard marginal cost–based system.

A second company, Flying Foods, employed a similar reporting format. This food processing company operates in five different markets and, like Fuchsia Fabrics, had set out its reporting in contribution style and, where possible, attributed overhead to each market-oriented business unit. The format adopted is illustrated in Table 3.2. The similarities with the Fuchsia Fabrics' reporting format are striking. Once again a contribution style format has been adopted and, again, the focus is on the identification of variable manufacturing costs and on those other overheads that can be

Table 3.2: Internal reporting format adopted at Flying Foods

	Local authorities	Farm products	Services	Healthcare	Catering & Wholesale
Sales revenue	X	X	X	X	X
Less Prime cost[a]					
Raw material	(X)	(X)	(X)	(X)	(X)
Direct labour	(X)	(X)	(X)	(X)	(X)
Packaging	(X)	(X)	(X)	(X)	(X)
Gross profit	X	X	X	X	X
Less Marketing cost	(X)	(X)	(X)	(X)	(X)
Selling cost	(X)	(X)	(X)	(X)	(X)
Distribution cost[b]	(X)	(X)	(X)	(X)	(X)
Controllable contribution	X	X	X	X	X
Less Manufacturing overhead	(X)	(X)	(X)	(X)	(X)
Administration overhead	(X)	(X)	(X)	(X)	(X)
Net profit	X	X	X	X	X

[a]At standard, standards are set annually (in October) and in general no intra-year revisions are made.

[b]Currently an allocation based on an analysis "every so often" (Paul, Flying Foods) "hope to [attribute it] on some sort of cost per drop, cost per case, . . . charges for stopping the lorry and a charge per case it's never going to be perfect, you can't charge per mile . . . its too complicated."

attributed to business units. At this company there is some interest in activity-based approaches for attributing overhead to business units and this is readily understandable, because 50% of management bonuses depend on achieving "controllable contribution" in the business units. (The other 50% depends on the overall profitability of the company.)

A third company, Elm Engineering, was very small (turnover about £1.2 million per annum) and therefore made no attempt to segment its business; a single P&L account was presented for the whole business. Here again there was much evidence of "contribution thinking". The reporting format is set out in Table 3.3. Cost of Sales is comprised of the cost of labour and material and, although termed "gross profit" the line calculated, as sales less cost of sales is, effectively, contribution. At Elm Engineering the Managing Director has consciously changed the internal financial reporting system, aiming to write off as much expense as possible each month. The Managing Director had had bad experiences with overvalued stock in larger companies and intended to ensure that

Table 3.3: Internal reporting format adopted at Elm Engineering			
			Notes
Sales		X	
Materials	(X)		Actual expenditure but adjusted for major stock changes
Direct labour	(X)		Actual expenditure including any overtime premium
Stock change			Always zero (form does not reflect current practice)
Consumables	(X)		Split out because the chief executive wants to see it
Carriage	(X)		
Cost of Sales		(X)	
Gross Profit		X	
Gross profit % sales		X%	performance measure used at board level, target is 40%
Salaries/Indirect labour	(X)		(Salaries and indirect labour shown separately)
Holiday pay	(X)		
Total Payroll		(X)	
Total other overhead		(X)	
Trading profit		X	

conservative policies were adopted. Even direct labour cost is written off as incurred.

When a fourth company presented its internal report in a similar fashion (see Table 3.4) it began to feel as though this might not be a coincidence. Flax Fans, a manufacturer of fans for ventilation of homes, offices and other public buildings is divided into two business units, "Fans Overnight" guaranteeing to have a fan available, on site, the next day and "Perfect Ventilation", the traditional "high specification" fan business. Once again this company organised its reporting in contribution style and, once again, marketing and selling overhead was attributed to the appropriate business unit.

This final company highlights an issue that was to become very important in the main part of our study. In the Flax Fans P&L, "Gross Profit" is calculated as "Net Profit" less "Manufacturing Overhead". This is not the conventional understanding of the accounting terms and their relationships that is to be found in CIMA handbooks and student textbooks. At first sight it may appear disconcerting or simply erroneous. Discussion with the Financial Director led us to interpret the P&L in the following way. Flax Fans assumes that certain costs can be attributed to the two "business units". The "Net Profit" is, in a sense, the net profit generated by the two businesses. We may have preferred a term such as "Direct Profit" to refer to this, but this was the terminology used in the company and the one that made sense to them. Gross profit is conventionally reported as sales less (all)

Table 3.4: Internal reporting format adopted at Flax Fans

	Fans overnight	Perfect ventilation
Sales revenue	X	X
Less Direct cost		
Materials	(X)	(X)
Direct labour	(X)	(X)
Contribution	X	X
Less Marketing overhead	(X)	(X)
Selling overhead	(X)	(X)
Net profit	X	X
Less Manufacturing overhead	(X)	(X)
Gross profit	X	X

manufacturing cost – so that striking a "Gross Profit" line after manufacturing overhead in Flax Fans also makes some sense. However, the problem with this is that this line is after variable selling costs and therefore is not, strictly, "gross profit" as conventionally defined.

The important methodological point is that meaning of the profit terms in Flax Fans was only identified as problematic once the detail of the P&L was available. The careful interrogation of accounting documents, with the guidance of the Financial Director who produced them, generated quite different meanings from those that would have been attributed if the terms used were taken at face value on the assumption that they corresponded with an agreed conventional usage. In the main part of the study we were to meet many such terminological problems. For example, in Chapter 4 we shall identify a company that uses the term "contribution" but does not apply it to the practices conventionally associated with the concept. Conversely, there are four companies where the term itself is not used but we conclude that the companies were actually following what would be conventionally defined as contribution reporting practices.

Learning from our initial pilot studies, we made two crucial decisions on method:

1. That the P&L format of each company must be available in order that they be included in the sample to be studied.
2. That postal questionnaire forms of research would be inappropriate for the study; instead we decided to conduct telephone interviews having first piloted an interview schedule in a further group of companies.

3.3   The secondary pilot companies

The requirement that companies provide a P&L *pro forma* had an important impact on the conduct of the research. The request for documentary evidence made an immediate, and unusual, demand upon Financial Directors and this seems likely to have deterred some hesitant companies from cooperating in the survey. Nevertheless, such was the importance we placed upon gaining access to the documentation that we were prepared to make this an absolute priority. We expected the benefits of having documentation to more than outweigh the inescapable limitations that would follow.

Anticipating some difficulty in gaining access to sufficient companies to form a useful sample, we decided to retain the original four cases acquired through the accounting–marketing inquiry. Where many cases are available it is possible to standardise procedures through pilot studies and then dispose of the pilot cases in order to make a "clean" survey of the main sample after the survey schedule has been designed. Given our anticipated difficulty in gaining a large sample we decided that there was more benefit in retaining the original companies on which we had, by this time, considerable information. However, in order to produce a standardised interview schedule we decided to approach six new companies where face-to-face interviewing would be carried out: Iris Instruments, Apricot Aeros, Marigold Medical, Pine Packaging, Apple Aerospace and Robin Rectifiers. These companies were approached because they were known to the research team and cooperation could be gained via personal contacts. No claim for "representivity" is made in regard to these companies. The interviews enabled the construction of the interview schedule to be used in the main body of the study (see Table 3.5) but, again, we did not dispose of the evidence gained from these and they are reported in our subsequent chapters.

3.4 The main study

For the bulk of companies in the study we decided upon a telephone interviewing procedure. Of course, all data gathering methods have their advantages and disadvantages; opportunities and constraints. The mobilisation of face-to-face interviews, or observation would probably have resulted in more in-depth "rich" data, though almost certainly with fewer companies.[15]

---

[15]In accounting research the standard for interview-based case studies appears to be three companies; the requirements of participant observation almost certainly would provide only one case.

Table 3.5: The Telephone Interview Schedule

1. Company structure
   - How many divisions, business units or subsidiary companies are there and what do they do?
   - Is there a MRP/ERP system?
2. Recent change
   - Has the company faced crises or major change?
   - Have there been any changes to internal reporting?
3. Internal reporting
   - What is the relative importance of the P&L and other reports?
4. Description of the P&L
   - Is the P&L analysed by product/market/business unit?
   - Are standard costs employed?
   - Are variances calculated?
   - Are they used?
   - Is there a contribution line?
   - Where do marketing and distribution costs appear?
   - Is overhead absorbed into products? – Is activity-based costing used?
   - How are stocks valued?
5. Internal versus external reporting
   - What, if any, adjustment is needed to the internal accounts to create external reports?
6. Performance measurement
   - Is financial performance important?
   - What measures are important?
   - Are bonuses paid for performance?
   - If so, how are they calculated?
   - Are actuals compared to budget?
   - Are forecasts prepared?
7. Decision making
   - How is financial information used for
   Pricing?
   Product mix decisions?
   Sourcing decisions?

On the other hand, the use of postal or email questionnaires would probably have achieved a much higher number of sample companies (and possibly more statistically sophisticated and rigorous sampling techniques) but would have delivered a more superficial description of each company. We have noted elsewhere (Dugdale and Jones, 1997) common problems with questionnaire surveys and problems that may arise in the interpretation of questionnaire data. Nevertheless, this does not mean that we reject the use of questionnaires.[16] We agree with Innes and Mitchell (1997) that a variety of methods are appropriate in accounting research and would add that this applies not only within a single research project (where it is typically termed "triangulation") but also between researches carried out within the research community.

In our experience, questionnaire surveys work well when either, but preferably both, of two conditions apply:

1. That researchers already have a relatively firm knowledge of the practices that are likely to be found in a substantial proportion of the surveyed companies, and a clear language, shared with respondents, that is capable of expressing these.
2. That practitioners in these companies have relatively firm, stable accounting practices of which they have good knowledge.

Under these circumstances, large-scale questionnaire surveys may be able to map the distribution of such practices that are already recognised by researchers and practitioners alike.

Neither of these two conditions applies to our current study. First, as we suggested above and will evidence later, there can be very considerable disparity – indeed a reversal – of academic/ researcher terminology and the corporate/practitioner vocabulary in different organisations. Thus, the possibility of asking clear questions that will result in certain answers in a non-discursive mode of enquiry (e.g. questionnaire) is compromised. Second, the pilot study suggested that forms of accounting are emerging so that they have not yet crystallised in the practices and discourses of companies/ practitioners in a manner that would allow simple questionnaire responses.

The telephone interview allows the conduct of research without the time-consuming physical necessity for travel, but still enables the inter-subjective creation of meaning and understanding (Dugdale and Jones, 1997; Jones, 1992). Of particular significance in this study is that a common base for discussion was established

---

[16]For example, we undertook a recent study of capital budgeting (Dugdale, *et al.*, 2003) that incorporated questionnaire findings from 159 companies (as well as telephone interviews in a sub-set of 39 of these).

in all cases by access to documentary material (the P&L pro forma) that is also available to the reader (see Appendix).

To conduct these telephone interviews we contacted companies drawn from the FAME database of medium and large companies in the South West of England.[17] These companies were approached via their Financial Directors (or Controllers) who were all personally identified. The importance of such "personalised" requests was established in our previous research. For example, in our study of capital budgeting (Dugdale *et al.*, 2003) the response rate for questionnaires from "personalised" mailings was a rather impressive 38%; from "anonymous" mailings (i.e. addressed to "Financial Director" or "Financial Controller") it was a rather poor 18%. Despite our having personalised all mailings for the CIMA project it took 348 initial mail shots, plus follow-up reminders, to gain the final 31 companies for the study. This very low response rate (9%) might be a function of many factors, including low level of corporate interest in the particular issues to be studied, but the most likely reason seems to us to be the requirement for P&L documents followed by telephone interviews. This style of research demands both that the company provides written evidence and that, ideally, the named person is the actual respondent so that that the request is not passed on to some other unspecified (but probably more junior) employee.[18] However, as we indicated earlier, we had decided that the value added by having the documentary evidence was sufficient to outweigh the problems of constructing the sample. The outcome was that 41 companies were eventually assembled as the sample (see Table 3.6). Basic information concerning the companies is summarised in Table 3.6.

The 41 companies that participated in the survey were drawn from a diverse range of manufacturing sectors. The companies are listed in the Contents of the Appendix to this report together with

---

[17]The region was chosen for pragmatic reasons. We might have wanted to visit the companies as part of this project. If not, we wanted to add to our collection of potentially cooperative companies, within easy access of the University of the West of England, for subsequent research projects.

[18]In practice we interviewed some-one who was not our primary contact in only one company.

Table 3.6: Companies in the survey			
Cases	*Interviews*	*P&L documents*	*No. of companies*
Original pilot	Face-to-face	YES	4
Secondary pilot	Face-to-face	YES	6
Main study	Telephone	YES	31
TOTAL			41

details of their business, sales revenue per annum, status (plc or private company) and ownership nationality.

The companies (mainly divisions of large groups) have sales revenue ranging from £1.5 to £500 million per annum with most (23 or almost 60%) in the range £15–£50 million per annum.

Typically the companies are part of publicly owned groups, although six companies (approximately 15%) are privately owned. The companies have diverse ownership. About half (21) have UK owners while 6 are under US ownership, 3 French, 2 Japanese and 2 German. There are also individual companies under Belgian, South African, Swedish, Canadian, Dutch, Norwegian and Finnish ownership.

The companies are difficult to classify by product, process or market. There are 2 large divisions of aerospace manufacturers and a smaller supplier to the aerospace industry. There are 4 companies that supply plastic pipes and mouldings and plasterboard to the building industry. Five more companies are connected with the building industry through supplying electric lighting systems, fire detection equipment, windows, shelving and fans respectively. There are suppliers of foam, non-woven fabrics and tyres to the automotive and domestic industries. Two companies specialise mainly in steel stockholding. Six companies are in process industries: beverages, food, chemicals, milk, leather and lubricants respectively. There are engineering companies: manufacturing precision parts in small batches, specialising in the manufacture of hydraulic valves and mass-producing aluminium cans. Manufacturers of equipment include specialists in dispensing equipment, eye testing and prosthetics for the disabled. Two companies manufacture electronic components. In short, the 41 companies are engaged in a wide range of manufacturing activity.

3.5   A concluding note on methods

The choice of methods always involves certain compromises and depends upon a balance of judgements made by the researchers. In the case of this study it was our view that the benefits of documentary evidence followed by focused telephone interviews was the most appropriate compromise in the light of the nature of the issues under study. However, we must note the limitations involved. Given the low response rate we were not able to "select" the companies surveyed following any techniques for "random" or "stratified" sampling. Thus the statistics produced from the study are not amenable to the standard techniques that apply to such samples. Even though in subsequent chapters we will indicate, for example, that 28 of our 41 companies employed contribution concepts in their internal reporting, and this could easily be represented as 68% of cases, this should not be taken to indicate that we are suggesting that two-thirds of UK manufacturing companies apply such concepts. There is no attempt in this report to assess the relative distribution of various accounting forms. Instead, what will be argued is that there are both *differences* in internal reporting practices (with companies showing significant variation in their accounting forms) and also *divergence* (with various directions – sometimes contradictory – being pursued by different companies). We believe that our 41 cases will convincingly establish this dual proposition, and allow an indication of the range across which it applies. We would also emphasise that it is only through the close interrogation of the detail of the accounting formats, in conjunction with the explanations offered by those who have constructed them, that we were able to portray the accounting practices of the companies in the way that we have. We ask that readers who may come to feel entrapped in the detail of the mass of data that will follow in subsequent chapters would bear in mind that it is only through the analysis of such detail that we can come to an understanding of the particularity – we might say idiosyncrasy – of contemporary developments in management accounting.

4

The Presentation of Financial Information: The Definition of "Contribution Margin"

4.1 Introduction

A major aim of the research was to gain insights into the ways in which manufacturing companies present financial information for internal management use. A key element of the research methodology was a request that participating companies provide a copy of their P&L format and, in this chapter, we present an analysis of the formats received.

A majority of companies in this study employ contribution concepts in their internal financial reporting. This is consistent with the pilot study discussed in the previous chapter and provides further evidence that manufacturing companies find the division of costs into "fixed" and "variable" components useful. Among the 41 companies, 28 employed contribution concepts in their reporting, 9 did not and in 4 companies the situation was unclear (see Table 4.1).

If our field study is representative of UK manufacturing companies then this finding is significant. It implies that contribution concepts are alive and well in UK manufacturing companies and raises questions about the, often presumed, domination of absorption costing methods. The implications of this finding are discussed at the end of the chapter.

First, however, we address issues of terminology. A key issue arises in the *definition* of "contribution" because many variations in terminology were encountered. After dealing with these terminological issues we discuss the formats and definitions used

Table 4.1: Contribution concepts in the 41 survey companies	
Financial presentation	*Number of companies*
Explicit use of contribution concepts	12
Explicit reference to contribution but P&L needed interpretation	3
Using contribution concepts but employing alternative terminology	4
Using contribution concepts but employing confusing terminology	9
Difficult to classify but possibly employing contribution concepts	4
Use of the term "contribution" but not defined conventionally	1
Explicitly gross profit or gross margin (not contribution) based	8

by those companies that employ contribution concepts before discussing possible implications for the "relevance lost" thesis of management accounting.

4.2 Issues of terminology

Explicit use of contribution concepts

Twelve companies employ contribution style formats using terminology that is consistent with textbook prescriptions. Examples include Shasta Ships (contribution struck after direct materials and subcontract, and labour costs); Forget-me-not Foam (contribution struck after materials, labour, transport and despatch); Primrose Packaging (contribution struck after materials, labour, maintenance and energy costs) and Fuchsia Fabrics (contribution struck after materials, labour, power/water and transport costs). For example:

Shasta Ships	*Forget-me-not Foam*
Turnover	Turnover
(Direct materials and subcontract)	(Materials)
(Production labour)	(Direct labour)
	(Transport and Despatch)
Contribution	Gross contribution

Explicit reference to contribution but P&L needed interpretation

Three companies (Flying Foods, Bluebell Building Products and Fir Films) refer to both "contribution" and "gross profit/margin" in their reports. At Flying Foods "gross profit" is struck after material, packaging and labour costs and "contribution" is calculated by the further deduction of selling and distribution costs. At Bluebell Building Products "gross margin" is struck after materials, labour and power with "contribution margin" after the further deduction of "other manufacturing costs". At Fir Films "gross contribution" is struck after standard material and labour costs and "gross margin" is struck after accounting for material and labour variances. Despite the insertion of gross profit/margin lines, these three companies employ contribution formats, refer to "contribution" and calculate lines in their P&Ls that accord with contribution concepts.

Using contribution concepts but employing alternative terminology

Four companies fall into this category. Although they do not use the term "contribution" there is little doubt that they are employing contribution style formats and describe these formats using appropriate language. Cherry Components refers to "direct profit" instead of contribution; Marigold Medical calculates "sales less material and labour margin %"; Tulip Tyres does not mention "contribution" but refers to its P&L as a "marginal income statement"; Rose Resins refers to "margin on variable cost" instead of contribution. There is little doubt that these companies are employing contribution formats and ideas; they simply choose alternative (but appropriate) terminology.

Using contribution concepts but employing confusing terminology

There are 9 companies in this group all providing examples of the difficulties of interpretation encountered during the research. There are classic cases at Everlasting Extinguishers and Aster Autovending where "gross margin" is calculated by deducting direct material and direct labour from sales revenue. Similarly, Heather Health Equipment strikes "gross margin" by deducting direct materials, direct labour and direct royalties from sales. Oak Oils reports an "operating margin" that might be more accurately termed "contribution"; "gross margin" is calculated as sales less material cost of sales and then variable costs deducted to yield "operating margin" ("operating margin" was consciously preferred over "contribution"). At Carnation Cans "manufacturing margin" is struck after deducting materials and variable sales costs from sales revenue. "Manufacturing margin" is also reported at Campion Catalysts but, as this company buys its product from other group subsidiaries, this line is also contribution margin. Honesty Hydraulics calculates "manufacturing profit" by deducting materials and labour from sales revenue. At Petunia Plastics, gross profit is calculated after materials, labour and "direct overheads". Our interviewee insisted that: "they're all variable, there's no fixed in there at all" so, again, this company was treated as reporting contribution under another name. And Elm Engineering also reports "gross profit" but our interviewee confirmed that manufacturing overhead is written off each month and, as it appears below gross profit, the gross profit line effectively reports contribution. These nine companies report gross profit, gross margin, operating margin, manufacturing margin and manufacturing profit but, in all nine cases, margin or "profit" is calculated in a manner consistent with the calculation of contribution. Examples:

Everlasting extinguishers	Honesty hydraulics
Total sales	Sales
(Direct material)	(Materials)
(Direct labour)	
————	————
Gross margin	Added value
	(Direct labour)
	————
	Manufacturing profit

In all these cases it is judged that the company is "really" using contribution ideas.

Difficult to classify but possibly employing contribution concepts

There are 4 companies that are not easily categorised. Larkspur Lighting might be classified as using contribution concepts because both labour and production overhead are written off as incurred and no overhead is included in the value of stock. However, Larkspur's P&L format strikes gross profit after deduction of labour, production overhead, transport and warehouse costs and does not include a contribution line at all. Iris Instruments is also difficult to classify because it includes a "material gross profit" line and, if materials were the only variable cost, this would effectively report contribution. On balance it was judged that the company gives greater weight to "profit before overheads", struck after the deduction of production overhead costs. Daffodil Dairy and Thyme Tanneries are difficult to classify because their monthly financial reports are generated by simple closure of the financial books of account. These companies might be seen as employing contribution ideas because overhead is (usually) written off as incurred. However, both companies employ broadly traditional P&L layouts with references to gross profit/margin (not contribution).

Use of the term "contribution" but not defined conventionally

One company, Daisy Drinks, refers to "contribution" but includes fixed expense in the calculation of product costs and reports "contribution margin" after deducting fixed manufacturing costs from sales. It is concluded that this company is not truly reporting contribution.

Explicitly gross profit or gross margin (not contribution) based

Eight companies are judged to be employing a gross margin style P&L without striking a line after variable costs either explicitly or implicitly. These companies refer to gross margin or gross profit and calculate it by deducting (full) manufacturing costs from sales revenue. Only one of these companies, English Enzymes, posed a classification problem, including distribution costs (as well as all production costs) in cost of sales.

General comments

Assessing how many companies are employing "contribution" concepts in their internal financial reporting is not easy. There is a wide range of practice with some companies conforming to an "ideal" type, calculating and naming contribution in conventional ways, while others use alternative terminology, often drawing on terms from financial reporting (especially "gross profit" and "gross margin") to label variants of contribution margin reporting.

Despite the difficulties involved, we believe that our broad conclusion that a majority of the companies taking part in the survey employ contribution formats is correct. Our main test in classifying a company as using contribution reporting is the existence of a line in the P&L derived as sales less variable costs, irrespective of how this line is named – and 28 companies met this test. Of those companies deemed to be employing contribution formats, there are eleven that use the terms gross profit or gross margin in their P&L accounts. Seven calculated contribution as sales less variable costs but named it gross profit or gross margin and four established a "gross profit" line before going on to calculate contribution after further expenses. (Three of these were the wholesalers/intermediaries, Cornflower Coated Steels, Oak Oils and Campion Catalysts where it may be traditional to quote gross profit as sales less material costs.)

The ubiquitous references to gross profit and gross margin by companies that employ contribution concepts might have led questionnaire surveys to underestimate the institutionalised use of marginal costs and contribution concepts in UK manufacturing companies. The issue is made more complicated by the fact that some companies use contribution concepts but name them differently; whilst others use the term "contribution" but do not follow what are conventionally understood as contribution reporting practices. In this study we conclude that 9 companies referred to gross margin, gross profit, etc. when contribution margin would be more appropriate and one company referred to contribution when gross margin/profit would be more appropriate. Without analysis of the P&L formats these companies might have been misclassified and this suggests that surveys may underestimate the extent of contribution reporting practices. This field study indicates that significant numbers of companies find the identification of variable costs useful and they distinguish between variable and fixed costs in their internal financial reporting.

4.3 "Contribution companies": The definition of contribution

The following analysis is based on scrutiny of the manner in which the 28 "contribution companies" define contribution in their P&L accounts (see Table 4.2). There is considerable

Table 4.2: Analysis of items deducted from sales in order to establish "contribution" (28 companies)	
Cost item	*Number of companies identifying the item as a variable cost*
Materials	28
Labour	21
Transport	7
(Variable) production costs	12
(Variable) selling costs	3

variation in the way that contribution is calculated in the survey companies.

Materials

All 28 "contribution companies" treat material costs as variable in the calculation of contribution. One manufacturing company, Tiger-lily Typing defined contribution as sales less *only* material costs. In this company "contribution %" is calculated as ". . . materials, packaging, all material costs, taken away from sales and expressed as a percentage." It was clear that this is important because our interviewee continued: "In this business this is quite a key indicator of how we're doing." And one "wholesaling" or intermediary, Campion Catalysts, undertakes no local manufacturing so its "gross profit" line, struck as sales less transferred in costs, is also simply sales less material costs.

All the remaining companies combine material costs with other variable costs in the calculation of contribution.

Labour

There are 7 companies, Tiger-lily Typing and Campion Catalysts mentioned above together with Oak Oils, Cornflower Coated Steel, Carnation Cans, Rose Resins and Poppy Plasterboard that do not include labour as a variable cost, calculating contribution as sales less combinations of materials, variable production costs, variable selling costs and transport. Campion Catalysts, Oak Oils and Cornflower Coated Steel are effectively wholesalers so the omission of labour is logical for them. And Rose Resins is a process manufacturer of resins so, again this seems sensible. Carnation Cans and Poppy Plasterboard are subsidiaries of French parents and follow their parents' format. When it was suggested that Carnation Cans' P&L format was "very carefully constructed", the response was: "You give us too much credit I think."

The remaining 21 companies treat labour as a variable cost and, with the exception of the seven companies just discussed, combine this with material costs in the calculation of contribution.

Variable production costs

A significant minority (11) identify particular production costs as variable in the calculation of contribution. The items of cost most usually treated as variable are power (5 companies), maintenance (3 companies), running costs (3 companies) and depreciation (3 companies). It might seem strange that depreciation should be included in the calculation of contribution but these companies referred to "direct" depreciation and to the write off of specific tools and fixtures. There were also companies that treated water and "consumable" costs as variable. One company specifically highlighted royalties as a "direct" cost.

Variable selling costs and transport costs

Few companies (3) include variable selling costs in the calculation of contribution although more (7) explicitly include transport costs in the calculation. One company (Rose Resins) includes both items in the calculation and the two subsidiaries of French parent companies, Carnation Cans and Poppy Plasterboard include variable selling costs and transport costs respectively in their calculations. In some companies "transport costs" is actually defined more widely than just transport and "distribution costs" would be more accurate. These companies were grouped together in order to simplify the presentation of results.

Summary

There are 2 companies that treat only materials as a variable cost and 11 that treat just materials and labour as variable costs. There are 5 companies that combine materials with other variable costs but treat labour as a fixed cost. The remaining 10 companies calculate contribution by treating material and labour costs as variable together with various combinations of variable production costs, variable selling costs and transport costs. Six deduct material, labour and variable production costs from sales. One (Forget-me-not Foam) deducts materials, labour and transport costs from sales. Three (Fuschia Fabrics, Tulip Tyres and Primrose Plastics) deduct materials, labour, variable production costs and transport costs from sales.

4.4 Changing financial systems in "Contribution" companies

Introduction

It is not so easy to trace the history of change in internal reporting. Many respondents left us with the impression that the formats we observed had been in place for some considerable time. However, our methodology was limited in that discussions were with a single company representative who, sometimes, had only been with the company for a limited period. We are therefore agnostic about the extent of change taking place in these companies. However, occasionally, we spoke to someone who clearly *did* know something about the history of financial reporting in the company. Sometimes the comments made were very enlightening.

Marigold Medical

The financial controller was very clear that: "Putting it politely, [he] couldn't care less about apportioning rent and rates and how much electricity goes into a product." (He also made some rather less polite comments about the absorption of overhead costs!) Our contact obviously thought deeply about the appropriate format for internal reporting because he had recently *introduced* labour into the calculation of his key performance measurement line, sales less materials and labour expressed as a percentage of sales. Prior to the change this had been calculated as sales less materials as percentage of sales. However, it had been necessary, in the recent past, to make 20% of the workforce redundant and this had persuaded our interviewee that labour should be treated as a variable cost for reporting purposes.

Tulip Tyres

At this company a conscious decision had been taken two years ago to adopt a marginal costing format. "We were just reviewing our business effectively and decided that we wanted our P&L to reflect more closely the way we made our decisions." The interviewee expanded on this by explaining how "direct profit" was calculated for each business unit: ". . . the marginal income less specific expenses for each of those market or business units". It was clear that this "direct profit" is key to running the business, reflecting the organisation structure with individuals responsible for each business unit and its direct profit. Overheads are apportioned to business units for other purposes but: ". . . we don't measure the management of those business units or markets at anything below direct profit."

Forget-me-not Foam

This company adopts a near classic contribution style format and, in the early part of the interview, it seemed that the adoption of a presentation that aligned with the interviewee's preference was a coincidence. However, it became clear that this was not the case. "It wasn't always this way. Basically what happened was in 1996 we had a change of group management, a Managing Director came in, and we basically sat down and went through what we felt could be measured in the business . . . I was a member of a team of people called Senior Finance Officers [that] said 'What are we going to do?' I piloted this certain format in our company and it was successful here and then they've basically extended it throughout the group and now everybody is using it. The thing is it's fairly simple you know it's not trying to over complicate things. I mean at the end of the day you know business is all about communication and you have to get that message across."

Elm Engineering

The managing director of this small company explained his concerns with traditional absorption costing very colourfully. He had had unfortunate experiences working in a large group (before a management buyout). Our interviewee said that, in that company, accounting practices resulted in: ". . . giving accountants far too much status because they're the only ones who know what's going on, because it's all bloody jargon and appalling decisions are made." He was clearly unhappy with notions of cost such as £80 or £90 per hour (including overhead): ". . . but that's how British industry ran itself and I'm afraid our group controller would come up with that crap today." This interviewee felt that the safest policy is to write off expenses as incurred.

4.5 The presentation of financial results and the "Relevance Lost" thesis

The finding that a majority of the companies in our sample employ marginal costing concepts is significant because it implies that many manufacturing companies do, in fact, follow long-standing academic advice by separating fixed and variable costs. Following the criticisms of Johnson and Kaplan (1987) there has been a tendency to assume that manufacturing companies, in thrall to the requirements of financial reporting standards, have concentrated on gross margin (sales less both fixed and variable manufacturing costs). Our study informs this debate by revealing that manufacturing companies might analyse fixed and variable costs but use the language of financial accounting (the ubiquitous references to gross margins) when describing this.

It is possible that the use of financial accounting terms has led to an underestimation of the number of companies employing contribution concepts. However, close reading of previous surveys reveals that our results are not necessarily inconsistent with these. Drury *et al.* (1993: 9), while broadly confirming the presence of full absorption costing in manufacturing companies, also reported that 52% of respondents "often/always" employed variable manufacturing cost in decision making. Drury and Tayles (2000: 50), surveying UK companies (not just manufacturing companies), found that 50% saw contribution as the most important measure for decision-making while 41% preferred a measure after arbitrary allocations or "bottom line" profit. Previous surveys are not, therefore, necessarily inconsistent with the conclusion that the majority of companies in our study institutionalise contribution ideas in their internal financial reporting.

This finding has implications for the "Relevance Lost" thesis. Johnson and Kaplan argued that financial reporting requirements dominate management accounting because they require the use of full manufacturing costs for stock valuation and these costs might be used for inappropriate purposes. If companies are not, in fact, using full manufacturing costs to calculate the key "margin" line in their P&L accounts, then financial reporting requirements do not appear to dominate their internal reporting. This was our initial conclusion.

However, matters are not so simple. In the next three chapters we explore further the methods used by the survey companies and a more complex picture emerges. In Chapter 5 we find that most companies use standard costs and, consistently, "contribution companies" tend to concentrate on variable cost variances for control. However, in Chapter 6 we find that many of the survey companies, while reporting a contribution line, prefer to report "bottom line" net profit on an absorption cost basis and, in this respect their, internal reporting *does* appear to be dominated by financial reporting regulations. In Chapter 7 we report the treatment of overhead, finding that most companies allocate overhead to products, business units, etc. although there is some evidence that contribution companies concentrate their attention on variants of product, market and business unit contribution.

Chapters 6 and 7 therefore provide some evidence of "absorption cost" thinking in those companies that report contribution. Nevertheless, overall, this study suggests that the Johnson and Kaplan argument that financial reporting requirements lead almost inexorably to (absorption) product costs that are flawed for decision-making purposes is suspect. Our evidence suggests that a significant proportion of companies concentrate on *variable* costs and the contribution generated by various segments of the business. We return to this debate after the analyses of product costing methods and stock valuation reported in Chapters 5 and 6.

Standard Costing and Variance Analysis

5.1 Introduction

As implied at the end of the last chapter there is an important inter-relationship between the presentation of financial reports and product costing systems. In principle one might expect companies that employ contribution margin reporting to emphasise variable or marginal costing while companies that report gross profit or gross margin (conventionally defined) might be expected to emphasise "full", absorption costing. These inter-relationships are important for our eventual conclusions. However, before studying these, it is convenient to report the extent of standard costing practice in the survey companies. This will facilitate analysis of the costing methods used by "contribution" and "non-contribution" companies in Chapter 6.

In a general way it was anticipated that manufacturing companies would employ standard costing methods. Standard costing has been advocated for almost a century and, theoretically, should help in "target" costing, controlling costs, supporting decision-making, evaluating managerial performance, facilitating management by exception and simplifying book-keeping entries. Previous surveys such as that of Drury *et al.* (1993: 35) have confirmed the widespread use of standard costs in manufacturing companies. However, since the 1980s the use of standards has come under attack because, it has been argued, excessive emphasis on variance analysis can be at odds with the new manufacturing philosophies of JIT production and TQM. Essentially, price concerns can mean insufficient attention to quality and delivery in material supplies and efficiency and overhead absorption reporting can encourage long production runs and stock building.

The majority (29 or over 70%) of companies in this survey employ standard costs. Thus this study is consistent with the results of other studies – most UK manufacturing companies do employ standard costs. In the first section, below, we analyse those companies that *do not* employ standards showing that this is often understandable given their particular businesses, ownership, etc. Then we review the practices of those companies that *do* set standards showing that most set standards for material and labour costs but fewer set standard overhead recovery rates.

We then turn to a key theme of this study by reviewing the extent to which standard cost of production and sales, together with related variances, is reported as part of internal P&L reporting. Several companies, although calculating standards, do not report variances as part of their internal P&L account. Thus, although standards might be calculated, this does not necessarily imply "full" standard costing systems and variance reporting. The extent and use of variance calculations is then considered and we conclude that, although variance analysis is important in some companies for particular items of cost, in general, variance analysis is not extensively deployed.

5.2 Analysis of companies not employing standard costs (Table 5.1)

Wholesalers

Four companies can be classified as largely "wholesalers" or intermediaries and two of these have important steel stockholding operations. Cornflower Coated Steels did not feel that standard costs were appropriate in its wholesaling business and ". . . every item of stock is costed at its purchase price". Similarly, the other steel wholesaler, Tiger-flower Tinplate, holds "bulk" at actual costs and establishes the precise margin (after material and distribution costs) on each sale.

Oak Oils, also largely an intermediary, purchases its product from "upstream" refineries at standard direct cost and continues to value product on this basis in its internal reporting. (For Oak Oils, the standard direct cost is the transfer price.)

Table 5.1: Analysis of the companies that do not employ standard costs (12 companies)

Nature of company/business	Number of companies
Wholesalers	4
Major contractors	4
"Traditional"	2
French/Belgium owned	2

The fourth company in this group, Campion Catalysts, also purchases its products (catalysts) from separate manufacturing operations (in Belgium, Luxembourg and the USA). This company pays the full cost of product including any variances incurred in the manufacturing companies. Perhaps this helps to ensure that ". . . the feeling across the company is to make sure that the variances are addressed." The consequence, for Campion Catalysts, is a purchase transfer price that reflects the actual cost of production.

Major contractors

There are four companies engaged in work to customer specification and one of these (Esther Enzymes) has single contracts that can be valued at as much as $1 million over a year. Although elements of standard costing can be detected in some of these companies they generally do not see standard costing techniques as particularly useful in their businesses.

Shasta Ships is in the business of maintaining and repairing ships; Sunflower Seals manufactures seals for the marine industry to customer specifications; Esther Enzymes produces pharmaceutical enzymes and Acacia Aerokit manufactures hydraulic servo valves for the aerospace industry. These companies use variants of project and works order accounting, booking actual costs incurred to projects or specific (works) orders. Although, generally, these companies do not feel that standard costing is appropriate to their businesses, at Shasta Ships our interviewee was interested in attempting to set standards for labour time for repetitive servicing contracts, in particular for routine servicing of ferries for major customers.

"Traditional" companies

There are two companies in this category, Daffodil Dairy and Larkspur Lighting. Both base their P&L reporting on simple closure of the financial books of account at the end of each month. These are not especially small companies (£18 and £25 million turnover per annum) but they are privately owned and have not developed sophisticated accounting systems. The P&L account at Daffodil Dairy was obviously extracted from the general ledger with headings that reflected this, while, at Larkspur Lighting our interviewee commented that: "It's one of the lowest levels of accounting that I've ever done to be honest." In both cases stock is often valued at material cost although at Daffodil Dairy, overhead might be included if stock holdings are abnormally large.

Companies with "gallic" parent companies

Two companies, Bluebell Building Products and Carnation Cans, are owned by multinationals based in Belgium and France respectively. These companies employ similar internal reporting formats with depreciation/amortisation charged at the foot of the P&L and neither company employs standard costs. Perhaps Gallic parent companies prefer to have actual costs reported and do not favour the use of standard costs. These companies also have some of the characteristics of the "traditional" companies mentioned above. Carnation Cans has grown rapidly in recent years (to its present turnover of £21 million per annum) and the parent company has pushed through systems changes. A SAP system has been installed (now regarded as an excellent system) and there is a group initiative to introduce ABC. However, our interviewee: ". . . really wants to push ahead with standard costing . . . because I think that will give us a much better handle on our costs and be much, much easier." At Bluebell Building Products, the computer system is rather old-fashioned and our interviewee felt that it did not merit the label MRP or ERP system. Both these companies value stock at something close to material cost and auditors have accepted this practice.

Comment

Failure to employ standard costs in 8 of these 12 companies can be understood because they are contractors or have limited manufacturing operations. In the other 4 companies, failure to adopt standard costing is less easy to explain. Perhaps, at Daffodil Dairy and Larkspur Lighting there has been no stimulus to change existing systems and, in the French- and Belgium-owned companies, the influence of their parents might be a factor.

In 3 cases interest was expressed in developing standard costs. At Tiger-flower Tinplate there is sufficient repetitive manufacturing activity for our interviewee to consider standard costs. At Shasta Ships, some contracts are sufficiently similar and frequent for our interviewee to consider the formal use of standard labour times and variances. And, at Carnation Cans, our interviewee was clearly in favour of the introduction of standard costs as a means of gathering information and controlling the business. It seems that, where companies concentrate on routine, repetitive activities they tend to become interested in setting standards and reporting variances. The extent of these practices in survey companies is considered in the next section.

5.3 The content of standard costs

All 30 companies that employ standard costing set standards for materials and most (26) also set a standard for the labour content of products (see Table 5.2). The most sophisticated analysis relates to material variances and the least sophisticated analysis to overhead variances. In fact "only" 60% (18) of the companies claim inclusion of manufacturing overhead in standard costs and 14 of these companies make no attempt to divide overhead into variable and fixed components.

In some companies the material "standards" are updated so frequently that one could argue they are not really "standards". Marigold Medical, Rose Resins, Heather Health Equipment and Primrose Plastics update their material cost standards *every month*

Table 5.2: Analysis of the content of standard costs (30 companies)

Item of cost	Number of companies including the item in standard cost
Materials	30
Labour	26
Variable production overhead	4
Fixed production overhead	2
Variable and fixed production overhead combined	14

so that they effectively report material costs at close to actual costs and, similarly, Forget-me-not Foam resets standards every quarter based on latest purchase order price. One might expect companies trading in volatile markets to be concerned that their material cost standards should be continuously updated. However, there is no real evidence that this is a factor in these cases. The 5 companies trade in "hygienic" storage units for the medical profession, synthetic resins, optical equipment for eye testing, plastic pipes and upholstery/automotive sound proofing and it is difficult to see any common influence. The apparently limited commitment of these companies to standard costing is explored in the next section.

5.4 The inclusion of standard costs in the profit and loss account

If a company sets standard costs for its products one might expect it to employ those standard costs in reporting expenses in its P&L presentation. Expenses would be reported at standard cost and then variances would also be reported in order to establish reported profit for the period and the whole report would facilitate management by exception. So runs one of the textbook justifications for the use of standard costs. However, the companies taking part in this survey provide only limited support for this use of textbook theory in practice. In this section we first discuss those companies that most obviously report *actual* costs (rather than standard costs). Then we move through the various combinations of standard and actual cost reporting and conclude with those companies that report expenses at standard together with an analysis of variances integrated into their financial reports (see Table 5.3).

Standards calculated but actual costs explicitly reported

Elm Engineering and Thyme Tanneries provide extreme examples of companies that calculate standard costs but do not employ them in their P&L presentations. Both these companies consciously ensure that actual costs are reported in their internal financial reports with standard costs calculated "off-line". Both companies had moved to this form of presentation in the recent past and could articulate their reasons for doing so (see Section 5.7).

Table 5.3: Analysis of the ways in which standard costs are (or are not) integrated with financial reporting (30 companies)

Use of standard costs in financial reporting	Number of companies
Standards calculated but actual costs explicitly reported	4
Standards calculated but actual costs implicitly reported	10
Material standard costs and associated variances reported but with "actual" labour and overhead costs	3
Difficult to classify as primarily standard or actual cost reporting	2
Standard costing and variances integrated into financial reporting	11

Two more companies, Pine Packaging and Petunia Plastics, are developing standard costs but do not yet employ them in financial reporting. Pine Packaging, producing only for confirmed orders, takes the sales value of *production* to P&L account. This means that the company does not account for finished goods stock and sophisticated costing is less important although an increase in the complexity of the product mix has led to interest in developing standard costs. At Petunia Plastics, a standard costing system was under development but: "I don't know whether we'll report on standard and then show variances . . . I'm just not sure whether they want that level of detail for the directors who are not financially sort of minded."

Four of the companies that set standard costs therefore do not employ them in their monthly performance reports, two have consciously chosen to do this while the other two might be moving in the opposite direction, attempting to integrate standard cost systems into internal reporting.

Standards calculated but actual costs implicitly reported

Another group of companies, while employing standard costs, appears to be intent on reporting actual costs. We noted above that 5 companies regularly update their material standards. In 4 of these cases (Marigold Medical, Heather Health Equipment, Rose Resins and Forget-me-not Foam), material "standards" are combined with reporting of *actual* labour and overhead costs. We conclude that these 4 companies effectively report actual costs. The clearest statement of policy came from Heather Health Equipment: "We run our systems on standard costs but by the time it gets through to these schedules its all actuals." (The fifth company, Primrose Plastics, although updating material standards regularly, in other respects, employs a fairly typical standard cost system.)

Additionally, there are 6 companies that set standards for materials but do not report material variances in their internal P&L reporting. These companies highlight actual costs in their internal reporting by "adding back" variances to costs at standard. Everlasting Extinguishers and Cherry Components add the material price variance to standard material cost – thus reporting something close to the actual material cost of sales.[19] Similarly, Peony Prosthetics and Poppy Plasterboard add back combinations of variable cost variances so that reported costs are at approximate actual values. And Campion Catalysts includes any variances in total cost of goods sold so that this line reflects actual, not standard cost. Flax Fans was one of the early "pilot" companies so full detail of the P&L account is not available. However, from the information available, it is judged that this company also effectively reports actual costs rather than standard costs plus variances.

Thus, a further 10 companies concentrate on actual (not standard) costs in their periodic reports by adjusting either their standards or form of reporting. All 10 of these companies also report *actual* overhead costs and this reaffirms their commitment to reporting actual costs.

Material standard costs and associated variances reported but with "actual" labour and overhead costs

There are 3 companies that include material costs at standard in their internal reporting together with material cost variances but then report labour and overhead costs at their actual value. Iris Instruments, Tiger-lily Typing and Aster Autovending fall into this

---

[19]In general, there are timing differences so that material cost at standard relates to sales while material variances relate to purchases and production so the reported material cost has some inconsistency in its calculation. However, at Heather Health Equipment a more sophisticated approach is adopted where material price variances are matched to the *use* of materials. "We roll variances into the balance sheet and release them over the deemed or calculated age of the stock."

category, essentially employing "textbook style" material cost standards and variances but then preferring to report actual labour and overhead costs.

Difficult to classify as primarily standard or actual cost reporting

There are 2 companies, Willow Windows and Shamrock Shelving that defy easy classification. These companies report labour and overhead costs at actual cost together with a total labour and overhead recovery line in their P&L accounts. These companies therefore report actual costs *and* a simple total variance (the difference between actual labour and overhead costs and labour/overhead recovered).

The presentations adopted by these companies are summarised below. The similarity is clear as both companies report labour and overhead costs incurred with a separate line for "labour and overhead absorbed" or "recovery". Notice that, despite their similarities, there are also differences between the two presentations. At Shamrock Shelving, cost of sales is not explicitly reported and the treatment of material costs is rather unclear. At Willow Windows, "adjusted" gross margin is not reported. Even where companies adopt fairly straightforward formats and terminology, their classification requires subjective interpretation of documentation and interview responses.

Willow windows	*Shamrock shelving*
Total sales	Sales total
(Cost of sales)	
Gross profit	Sales gross profit total
Materials variances	
	Recovery
Direct labour cost	Labour costs
Overhead incurred	Utilities/scrap
	Operations salaries
	Operations overheads
Labour and overhead absorbed	
	Gross margin
Distribution costs	
Administration expenses	
Operating profit	

Standard costing and variances integrated into financial reporting

Turning finally to the companies that appear to employ standard costs and report a range of variances. These 11 companies fall into two clear groups, those that employ standard direct costing systems and those that employ standard absorption costing systems. The standard direct costing companies are Flying Foods, Fuchsia Fabrics, Tulip Tyres, Fir Films and Primrose Plastics. The standard absorption costing companies are Apple Aeros, Honesty Hydraulics, Holly Health Furniture, Robin Rectifiers, Daisy Drinks and Apricot Aeros. Unlike the companies described above, these companies are closer to textbook stereotypes and relatively easy to classify.

General comment

Of 30 companies that calculate standard costs, there are 17 companies that do not report standard costs and variances in their P&L account or report only a limited subset of (materials) variances. We therefore judge that over 50% of the "standard costing" companies seem more interested in seeing *actual* costs reported in the prime financial report – the P&L account. Pine Packaging, Everlasting Extinguishers, Marigold Medical, Petunia Plastics, Rose Resins, Campion Catalysts, Elm Engineering, Poppy Plasterboard, Heather Health Equipment, Cherry Components, Thyme Tanneries, Forget-me-not Foam, Flax Fans and Peony Prosthetics aim to report *all* their costs at actual values. Additionally, Aster Autovending, Tiger-lily Typing and Iris Instruments report only material costs at standard. We conclude that, in this field study, although about 75% of companies employ standard costs, over half of these prefer to report actual costs in their P&L reporting.

5.5 The use of variance analysis

Virtually all of the 30 companies that employ standard costs calculate variances (see Table 5.4). The single exception is Petunia Plastics where (some) standard costs have been established but variances are not yet routinely calculated. There is also one

Table 5.4: Analysis of variances calculated (29 companies)

Variance calculated	Number of companies
Material price	25
Material usage	20
Total material (only)	4
Labour rate	10
Labour efficiency	11
Total labour (only)	15
Variable overhead rate	1
Variable overhead efficiency	1
Total variable overhead (only)	5
Fixed overhead expenditure	3
Fixed overhead volume	3
Total fixed overhead (only)	7

company, Shasta Ships, that, although not explicitly employing standard costs, is interested in the time taken to carry out standard repairs (typically on ferries) and compares actual time taken to the standard estimates. Whether Shasta Ships is really a standard costing company is debatable, its methods are probably typical of contracting companies that routinely compare labour time estimates to actual time taken.

Materials variances

Of the 30 companies that set standards for materials, 29 calculate material variances and many (20) calculate both price and usage variances. The other 9 companies calculate only a single material variance and 4 of these (Fir Films, Aster Autovending, Heather Health Equipment, Flax Fans and Iris Instruments) referred only to material price variances.

Of the 20 companies that calculate both material price and usage variances some mentioned further analysis:

◆ Five confirmed that they specifically report scrapped materials.
◆ Three – Daisy Drinks, Robin Rectifiers and Honesty Hydraulics – said that material exchange rate variances are calculated so the variance due to "non-exchange" effects can be isolated. (The exchange rate variance is calculated by establishing a standard

exchange rate when the material standard is set. This allows the impact of any difference between standard and actual exchange rates on total purchase price to be calculated.)

◆ There is little interest in material mix variances although the process manufacturer, Daisy Drinks, does calculate these variances together with materials price variance due to exchange rate fluctuation.

◆ One company, Willow Windows, explicitly referred to the separate analysis of one element of material expenditure. This company reports the material variance for glass separately from other material variances.

Labour variances

Most (26) of the standard costing companies also calculate labour variances. Ten establish both labour rate and efficiency variances; one (Shasta Ships) reports labour efficiency only; 14 report a single labour variance (subsuming both rate and efficiency variances) and one, the process manufacturer, Daisy Drinks, reports a combined labour and overhead variance. A few of these companies mentioned further analysis:

◆ One company, Campion Catalysts, analyses downtime.
◆ Willow Windows calculates labour mix variances.
◆ Apricot Aeros and Honesty Hydraulics establish "method variances". These arise as a sub-analysis of the efficiency variance if the standard production method changes.

Thus most of the standard costing companies report labour variances and only 4 (Petunia Plastics, Flying Foods, Tiger-lily Typing and Poppy Plasterboard) do not. Petunia Plastics does not (yet) calculate any variances while the other 3 companies calculate material variances but report labour at actual cost in their P&L.

There was an interesting comment from our interviewee at Apple Aeros where an extensive lean manufacturing initiative was underway. The withdrawal of efficiency variances had been considered because of the well-documented deficiencies of variance analysis in lean manufacturing environments. However, this had run into resistance from shop-floor supervisors who wanted to retain efficiency variances for management information and control purposes.

Variable overhead variances

Six companies calculate variable overhead variances although only one of these, Shamrock Shelving, analyses this variance into rate and efficiency components. The remaining five companies, Fuschia Fabrics, Tulip Tyres, Rose Resins, Esther Enzymes and Primrose Plastics, establish a single variable overhead variance. The use of variable overhead variances is therefore limited. In 5 of these companies, interest in variable overhead standards and variance reporting is consistent with their employing variants of contribution and marginal costing presentations.

Fixed overhead variances

Ten companies calculate "fixed" overhead variances, 7 of these reporting a single total variance. We include inverted commas round "fixed" because, in several of these companies, no attempt is made to separate variable from fixed overhead and therefore the "fixed" overhead variance is more accurately a "total" (manufacturing) overhead variance.

Only 3 companies analyse overhead variance into spend and volume components and none analyse the overhead volume variance into its capacity and efficiency elements.

Comment

We have shown that, if a company sets standards, then it is likely to calculate both material and labour variances. So, although there is a tendency for "standard costing" companies to report *actual* costs in their P&Ls, they nevertheless calculate material and labour variances. We note, however, that this variance analysis is often not particularly sophisticated. Although many companies calculate material variances, only 10 (of 30 standard costing companies) report a "full set" of material price/usage and labour rate/efficiency variances.

Our conclusion that variance analysis is often selective is reinforced by consideration of the overhead variances that the companies use. Only 14 companies (slightly less than 50% of those employing standard costs) report overhead variances and, in almost all cases, the reporting is limited. Ten of the 14 report only a single overhead variance (4 calculate a variable overhead variance, 6 calculate a "fixed" overhead variance). One company reports both fixed and variable overhead variances but does not analyse them into their components. Two companies analyse "fixed" overhead variance into spend and volume elements but do not report variable overhead variances. And just one company reports a "full set" of variable and fixed overhead variances analysed into rate, efficiency, spend and volume components.[20]

No company analyses overhead volume variance into capacity and efficiency elements and this reflects the findings of Drury *et al.* (1993: 37): "Approximately 80% do not compute fixed overhead volume capacity and efficiency variances." Drury *et al.* go on to question why these variances are still examined by professional bodies when they find so little favour with both practitioners and academics. Armstrong (1995) has also commented on the fixed overhead volume variance, colourfully describing it as "hovering on the verge of meaning". One of our conclusions will be that, after many years of theoretical developments, manufacturing companies have tended to opt for relatively simple financial presentations that avoid complex theory.

5.6 The purposes of standard costing

If this study is representative, the use of standard costs is still prevalent in manufacturing companies in the twenty-first century. There were a number of references to variances being useful, while there were also a number of less than complimentary references. A flavour of the comments made is provided by the following extracts, set out more or less from the most to the least favourable.

♦ At Holly Health Furniture "... we do calculate all the variances and we do use them." Purchase price variances were receiving particular attention following the introduction of a global purchasing function.

♦ At Shasta Ships, labour productivity is calculated and "... the calculation might be wrong, but the trends are right."

---

[20]This company went into liquidation as the project was nearing completion.

- At Tulip Tyres material, labour and variable overhead variances are calculated and used "in a balanced way" alongside other performance indicators.
- At Shamrock Shelving, improvements in the standard costing system are planned so that labour, variable overhead and fixed overhead variances can be separated. Our interviewee wanted to update standards annually but changing steel prices makes this problematic because the system is used for estimating.
- At Pine Packaging, "full" standard costs are under development – even including selling and administration expenses. Here the primary aim is to assess the profitability of different elements of an increasingly complex product mix.
- At Willow Windows, labour variances are analysed in detail, including rate, efficiency and mix components, and reported independently of the P&L account. This company also provides an example of the "unusual" use of standards as "full" manufacturing standard costs are based on outdated overhead rates, set when product volumes were significantly lower. This ensures that "full costs" and hence transfer prices are not reduced and aims to ensure that all parts of this vertically integrated group generate profits.
- At Cherry Components, material variances are seen as useful but the other variances are not reported. "I personally have got a very detailed matrix of cost but the management don't use it directly . . . I keep this information in the background." At this company, standards have not been changed for two years because volumes have fallen and overhead recovery rates would increase if they were recalculated. Maintaining old standards was the simplest way to avoid overstating the cost of products.
- At Poppy Plasterboard, materials variances are important and, asked if they are reported separately: "They are indeed . . . we report the variances in total by area . . . it's split down into price and usage by area as well." However, at this company, the use of variance analysis is limited to only materials as labour and overhead are written off as incurred and no variances are calculated for these items of cost.
- At Rose Resins, a sophisticated standard costing system included as many as 200 separate recovery rates (for the many production vessels). However, for control purposes: ". . . the

ones we look at with managers are really the material usage variances . . ." (At this company there are "recipes" for each of the products and control of materials used is important.) Despite the sophistication of overhead recovery variances they are not used in management reports and ". . . that's something we look at within the Finance Department and that's really more for stock valuation basis . . ."

◆ At Fuchsia Fabrics, standards and variances became more important when top management was interested, so the appointment of a production-oriented Managing Director meant that labour variances became important: ". . . yes, very much so, used as a tool in the business." However, "total" product costs seemed to have little value except for stock valuation: ". . . and the computer does all of that . . . [but] . . . nobody used to take any notice of them . . . it is just purely for us accountants to value stock."

◆ At Tiger-lily Typing, standard costing seemed to be partly driven by the computer system: ". . . the system does calculate . . . direct labour and efficiencies and manufacturing variances and everything. The only thing is . . . we still haven't got to grips with it." Our interviewee went on to comment that there was confidence in the purchase price variance, ". . . that is the one the system can't screw up on us."

◆ Peony Prosthetics was somewhat similar. Standards are set for materials and labour and the MRP system calculates price and usage/efficiency variances automatically. However, the use of these variances was obviously limited and referring to the material variances our interviewee commented: "Various accounts could fall into that almost by accident and I don't ever recall anyone ever discussing that with me." And, because standard labour times had not been updated: "We don't trust labour variances sufficiently to pay much attention to them actually."

◆ At Thyme Tanneries, variances are calculated but only as an indication of trends and standards are used to inform pricing: ". . . almost the only purpose now."

◆ At Elm Engineering the Managing Director, based on previous experience where stock had been over-valued was scathing: "Standard costing and variances can bite you on the arse at the end of the year when you find you have shortfalls."

Comment

These companies provide a range of views on the use of standard costs and variances. There are companies that use fairly sophisticated systems and are content that the variances reported are helpful in planning and controlling their businesses. There are also companies that employ standards in slightly "unusual" ways in order to achieve certain aims. Willow Windows and Cherry Components provide interesting and contrasting examples. Both these companies had maintained standard costs based on outdated overhead recovery rates, the former in order to ensure that costs do not fall, thus affecting transfer prices, the latter to ensure that costs do not rise, thus creating a problem by valuing stock above its net realisable value.

There are companies that employ variances but very selectively. Poppy Plasterboard and Rose Resins regard *materials* variances as important but neither is particularly interested in standards and variances for other items of cost. At Poppy Plasterboard, actual labour and overhead costs are simply written off as incurred while, at Rose Resins, standards for labour and overhead are of interest only to aid in valuing stock. Fuschia Fabrics provides a similar example where *labour* variances could be important but overhead standards are used only to aid in adjusting the value of stock.

Tiger-lily Typing and Peony Prosthetics provide two examples of companies that seem less than enthusiastic about the use of standards. At both companies it seems that variance analysis is more driven by the MRP systems installed than by management intent. Although Tiger-lily Typing does see merit in the materials price variance, both companies seem to have sceptical views of the value of standards and variances.

And, more extreme again, are the positions taken by Thyme Tanneries and Elm Engineering. At Thyme Tanneries the decision to discontinue reports based on standard costing was taken because it simply led to reconciliation difficulties with the financial books of account. And there is no doubt that, at Elm Engineering, the managing director has a rather jaundiced view of the value of standard costing and overhead absorption. These examples are dealt with in more detail in the next section.

5.7 Changing financial systems in standard costing companies

The last two companies, Thyme Tanneries and Elm Engineering, provide examples of companies that now regard standard costing and variances as peripheral to their operations and financial reporting. In both companies, standard costing systems still exist but there are serious reservations.

At Elm Engineering the managing director commented:

> John [the management accountant] ... has a standard costing base which tends to try to use factory overheads. But there's some scepticism on my part as to whether it's worth the paper it's written on ...

Although the system was designed to permit the recovery of overhead, this facility was no longer used. In fact the managing director had gone further, referring to labour costs:

> you've under priced the bloody thing in the costs ... I fell out [in a] previous existence with an accountant over this ... So now I have a strategy that says we will consider that labour is an overhead in terms of accounting monthly. Write it all off.

There is little doubt that, at this company, the standard costing system had been simplified. Previous experiences had led the managing director to distrust accounting stock valuations and he was now only prepared to accept changes in the material content of stock on a month-to-month basis.

A similar story emerged at the leather manufacturer, Thyme Tanneries. The respondent reported that, in the past 18 months the company had moved away from "operating statements" and variance analysis and now emphasised the monthly *financial* accounts "as our standard". Variance analysis was still undertaken but: "... we don't use it really as part of our major internal reporting. It's still there for sort of trend purposes ..." At this company basing the monthly reports on the financial ledger accounting was quicker and more reliable. Pressed on the specific reasons for problems with the operating statement the respondent continued:

> And costing stock reconciliations were becoming very difficult [with] standard costing methods ... We got to the stage of

[reconciling] operating results and using the stock adjustment line as a balancing figure to financial. So if that was the case . . . what's the point in doing it in the first place when all you're doing is making them the same?

These companies provide extreme examples of companies that, though experienced in the calculation and use of standard costing variances, no longer find them particularly useful. There are though several examples of companies that clearly still find variance analysis useful for particular items of costs and depending upon the particular needs of the business. There was some evidence that the approach to variance calculations and their use had changed in some companies. At Honesty Hydraulics, a comprehensive range of variances is calculated and, at one time, there would have been an inquest into any adverse variances. This monthly ritual had become an "academic exercise – an industry in itself." Now a more proactive approach is adopted and set piece confrontations avoided.

5.8 Concluding comments

Analysis of the use of standard costing and variance analysis in the survey companies reveals a mixed picture. Most of the companies that one would expect to employ standard costing systems do so. Where companies choose not to use standard costing systems, in several cases there are understandable reasons based on the nature of their business.

However, we do not conclude that standard costing and variance analysis is extensively employed in the survey companies. At the extremes there are examples of companies that are just setting up standard costing systems (Pine Packaging and Petunia Plastics) and companies that have more or less stopped using their standard costing systems (Elm Engineering and Thyme Tanneries). Between these two extremes there are a number of companies that employ standard costs and variances for particular items of cost. Most companies set standards for material and labour costs and there are examples of companies taking a particular interest in material and labour variances. Material price variances can be important and, in some companies (such as Rose Resins and Daisy Drinks) material usage variances are also important. Slightly fewer companies report labour variances and these might be reported in total rather than being split into rate and efficiency components. Nevertheless, here again, there are examples of companies, such Shasta Ships and Fuschia Fabrics that see these variances as important aids in managing their businesses.

It is in the calculation and use of overhead variances that the results are more surprising. Six companies calculate only variable overhead variances and, in five of these, their interest in variable costs is consistent with a preference for contribution or variable cost style P&L presentations. Just ten companies (33% of companies employing standard costs) report "fixed" overhead variances, only three of these split the overhead variance into spend and volume components and none analyse this last variance into capacity and efficiency elements.

If the survey companies are representative, standards and variances for variable elements of cost are important in some companies but treatments of standards for "fixed" overhead often seem to be oriented to stock valuation issues rather than to business management. This general observation is consistent with the findings of the previous chapter that reported a significant number of companies employing contribution and variable costing concepts in their financial reporting. The interaction of costing systems and the presentation of financial information is the subject of the next chapter.

Interaction of Profit Reporting
and Costing Systems

6.1 Introduction

The last two chapters analysed, first, the use of contribution concepts in financial reporting and, second, the use of standard costing in the survey companies. There is, of course, likely to be an interaction between these two themes. Companies that emphasise contribution reporting are expected to emphasise marginal product costs, writing off manufacturing overhead as a period cost. Companies that emphasise gross profit or gross margin reporting are expected to establish "full" manufacturing costs that include manufacturing overhead.

This chapter addresses these issues. In the next two Sections, 6.2 and 6.3, we consider the 28 "contribution-oriented"[21] companies and analyse their methods of product costing. Because the existence of standard costing systems makes it easier to determine how product costs are compiled, we consider these companies first. Then we turn to contribution companies that do not employ standard costing systems.

After dealing with contribution companies we consider the costing systems employed by the 9 "gross profit/margin" companies. Again we deal first with those that use standard costing (Section 6.4) and then those that do not (Section 6.5). Finally, we turn to those 4 companies that were difficult to classify in Section 4.2 and consider whether the costing methods employed throw any further light on the methods they use in reporting financial information.

Our conclusion is that companies employ broadly consistent methods; those emphasising contribution focus on marginal or variable product costs and those emphasising gross profit/margin calculate full manufacturing costs. However, this does not mean that the "contribution companies" employ marginal costing systems as defined in the textbooks. Almost invariably they employ an "adjustment" line in the P&L so that net profit is stated in accordance with financial reporting requirements.

---

[21]These are the companies that, in Section 4.2, were identified as explicitly or implicitly using contribution concepts, even though, in a number of cases, the terminology employed could be confusing. It does not include the four "unclear" companies that might be employing contribution concepts.

6.2 The contribution concept combined with standard costing

We begin our analysis by analysing the 20 "contribution companies" that also employ standard costs. Analysis of Table 6.1 reveals that, consistent with their marginal costing principles, 9 of these companies set standards only for variable costs. Surprisingly, given their supposed contribution orientation, the other 11 companies set standards for fixed production overhead, either in its own right or jointly with variable production overhead. However, the "Comment" column in Table 6.1 reveals that most of these companies use their "full" standard costs to make a P&L adjustment so that net profit is reported on an absorption-costing basis. Analysis of the *variances* reported reveals that these almost always relate only to elements of variable cost and this is consistent with financial reporting based on marginal cost principles.

The following discussion concentrates first on the 11 companies that set full product costs, then on the 9 companies that set variable product costs.

Eleven companies that combine contribution reporting with "full" standard costs

Two of these 11 companies, Pine Packaging and Cherry Components, are exceptional. At Pine Packaging, interest in standards is driven by a desire to analyse the profitability of its product mix. The costing system is, at present, completely decoupled from financial reporting because this company does not need to value finished goods stock, treating goods as sold as soon as they are made. Cherry Components follows the traditional (full cost) approach to stock and cost of sales valuation. However, this company is regarded as contribution-oriented because of the sophisticated calculation and reporting of "direct profit" as an integral part of its P&L.

The remaining 9 companies employ overhead recovery rates to establish "full" product costs. *However*, the main use of this information is as a means of valuing stock. Two of these companies, Elm Engineering and Petunia Plastics, make stock valuation adjustments only on an annual basis while the other 7 companies

Table 6.1: Standard costs in companies employing the contribution concept (20 companies)

Company	Standards set	Variances calculated	Comment
Pine Packaging	Material, Labour, Overhead	None yet reported	Standard costs not linked with financial reporting – used instead to indicate product profitability
Tiger-lily Typing	Material,Labour	Material, Labour	
Fuschia Fabrics	Material, Labour, Variable overhead, Fixed overhead	Material, Labour, Variable overhead	Fixed overhead recovery rates used to establish stock values and overhead adjustment in the P&L
Peony Prosthetics	Material, Labour	Material, Labour	
Poppy Plasterboard	Material	Material	
Flax Fans	Material, Labour	Material, Labour	
Forget-me-not Foam	Material, Labour	Material, Labour	
Primrose Plastics	Material, Labour, Variable overhead, Fixed overhead	Material, Labour, Variable overhead	Fixed overhead recovery used to make adjustment for overhead in stock. Group had not wanted this – now IAS are causing its more widespread introduction
Flying Foods	Material, Labour	Material, Labour	
Fir Films	Material, Labour	Material, Labour	
Cherry Components	Material, Labour, Overhead	Material, Labour, Overhead	Variances kept in background. P&L format shows the "direct profit" related to the sales value of production
Marigold Medical	Material, Labour	Material, Labour	
Tulip Tyres	Material, Labour, Variable overhead, Fixed overhead	Material, Labour, Variable overhead	Full absorption costing in parallel with "textbook" direct costing. A "whole cost adjustment" *below* the net profit line in the P&L

(Continued)

Table 6.1: Standard costs in companies employing the contribution concept (20 companies)—cont'd

Company	Standards set	Variances calculated	Comment
Rose Resins	Material, Labour, Overhead	Material, Labour, Overhead	Material usage variances are important for managers; the rest are useful in Finance for stock valuation
Everlasting Extinguishers	Material, Labour, Overhead	Material, Labour	Material price and usage and "total" labour variances reported. Overhead recovery useful in valuing overhead in stock adjustment
Aster Autovending	Material, Labour	Material, Labour	
Honesty Hydraulics	Material, Labour, Overhead	Material, Labour	Material and labour variances seriously used. A WIP adjustment is made for overhead in stock
Elm Engineering	Material, Labour, Overhead	Material, Labour	Managing Director ensures that labour and overhead are written off as incurred
Petunia Plastics	Material, Labour, Overhead	Variances not (yet) calculated	Actual costs reported; standards needed for year-end stock valuation
Heather Health Equipment	Material, Labour, Overhead	Material, Labour	Overhead recovery rates used for monthly "overhead in stock" adjustment

make a P&L adjustment *every month* and so ensure that reported net profit in their management accounts is in line with financial reporting requirements.

At Fuschia Fabrics, our interviewee commented: ". . . and the computer does all of that . . . [calculates fully absorbed costs] but nobody used to take any notice of them . . . it is just purely for us accountants to value stock." That our interviewee was less than enamoured on this adjustment was clear from his comment that: "overhead in stock movement . . . used to confuse the hell out of everybody . . . If stocks went up you had a credit to the P&L and if stocks went down, you had a debit to the P&L. So, of course, when we needed some profit, we built some stock." Similarly, at Rose Resins the MRP system calculates variances automatically based on the standard value of product transferred to finished goods. However, only material variances are useful in managing the business, and other variances: ". . . we look at in the Finance Department and that's really more for stock valuation . . ."

The experiences of two more of these companies, Primrose Plastics and Tulip Tyres, are noteworthy.

Primrose Plastics is a subsidiary of a group based in the Netherlands and there had been pressure from headquarters to cease the practice of adjusting the P&L for movement of overhead in stock. The parent company would have preferred stock to be valued at variable cost only. However, the projected introduction of international accounting standards had caused a change in policy, and other members of the group are now considering the introduction of a stock adjustment line.

Tulip Tyres provides a textbook example of marginal cost–based reporting together with an adjustment to profit to take account of changes in the value of fixed production overhead in stock. This company runs a full standard costing system including variances for material, labour and variable overhead. In addition, the inclusion of fixed overhead in product standard cost allows an adjustment for the monthly change in overhead in stock. However, unlike the other companies, this adjustment is struck *after* net profit has been established on a marginal cost basis. Thus Tulip Tyres reports profits under both marginal and absorption costing systems and there is no doubt that this company sees the marginal cost approach as the more valuable for management information and control purposes.

Our analysis demonstrates that, where contribution-oriented companies include overhead recovery in their product standards, they usually use the information so generated as a means of valuing stock. Most of these companies ensure that reported profit is compatible with financial regulations even though they adopt contribution formats in presenting financial information. And most of these (9 from 11) ensure that the monthly management accounts report "financial reporting" net profit. One of these 9 (Tulip Tyres) reports net profit on *both* marginal and absorption costing bases. Even though these companies base their reporting on marginal cost principles the influence of financial reporting regulations appears in their desire to report "full absorption" net profit on a regular, monthly basis.

Nine companies that combine contribution reporting with "marginal" standard costs

Given that those companies that set standard (fixed) overhead recovery rates use them mainly for stock valuation one might wonder how the 9 companies that *do not* set such rates cope with the problem of valuing stock.

Although not referring to the use of standard overhead recovery rates, at Tiger-lily Typing our interviewee did refer to MRP-based calculations for overhead adjustment and it is likely that this company adopts a similar approach to those discussed above.

Adjustments are also made at Poppy Plasterboard, Flax Fans, Flying Foods and Fir Films. However, at these four companies, the adjustment is made only annually so these companies operate on a marginal costing basis from month to month throughout the year. (In making annual adjustments these 4 companies adopt similar policies to Elm Engineering and Petunia Plastics discussed above.) Where an adjustment is made on an annual basis the need for overhead recovery standards is reduced because the adjustment can be treated as a "one-off" exercise. At Marigold Medical our interviewee adopted a similar approach, making an adjustment from time to time because he "couldn't be bothered" writing a journal for the adjustment every month.

At Forget-me-not Foam our interviewee had introduced an adjustment for overhead in stock. However, he very clearly did not wish to make this adjustment.

> I will be honest, I didn't want to do any overhead absorption at all and we didn't until last year because we were forced to do so by the auditors . . . I have to say I am not a fan of overhead absorption and even in financial reporting, as you probably gather, so therefore I didn't do it for a number of years. But we did over the last 18 months or so and you do get a fluctuation in your profitability because of it which I think is a bit spurious to be honest but there you go.

At Peony Prosthetics our interviewee had a similar attitude but had managed to avoid the introduction of an adjustment for the value of overhead in stock. Asked whether this caused a problem with auditors our interviewee responded: "We've just finished that process and no it didn't actually . . . well it's been done like that for the last god knows how many years and it's been alright in the past so we'll assume it's all right again."

The last company in this group is Aster Autovending. At this company the P&L includes a line for adjustment of overhead in stock but our interviewee, who had been with the company only a short length of time, was unable to expand on its use. In her experience, there had been no entries to this account and this suggested that the policy might be to make year-end adjustments.

Summary

This analysis indicates that, although a significant number of companies might like to see financial information compiled in accordance with marginal costing precepts, typically, they make an adjustment for the value of overhead in stock so that reported profit complies with financial reporting regulations.

There are 11 companies that employ "full" standard costs and 9 of these employ their standard costing systems to make adjustments to their financial reports so that *monthly* reported net profit is on an absorption cost basis. One of these 9 companies (Tulip Tyres) reports monthly net profit on *both* marginal and absorption bases.

The other 2 companies have "full" standard costs but make their P&L adjustment only annually.

There are 9 companies that employ "marginal" standard costs. Again most of these make adjustments so that their reported net profit complies with financial reporting regulations. However, fewer of these companies make the adjustment on a monthly basis. Five make an adjustment only annually so that in these companies, month to month, net profit is reported on a marginal cost basis. Additionally, Marigold Medical makes the "overhead in stock" adjustment infrequently so that month-to-month net profit is marginal cost based.

Tiger-lily Typing and Forget-me-not Foam seem to make monthly adjustments for the value of overhead in stock although this clearly stuck in the throat of our interviewee at Forget-me-not Foam.

Finally, one "standard marginal costing company" bases its external reporting on stocks valued at marginal cost, auditors allow this because it is consistent with previous practice and, probably, because the value of stock is not material to the reported results.

Table 6.2 summarises the interaction of contribution reporting and standard costing.

Table 6.2: Analysis of methods used by 20 "contribution companies" that employ standard costs			
	Companies making monthly adjustments to P&L	Companies making annual adjustments to P&L	Companies making no adjustments to P&L
Standards for variable costs only (9 companies)	2	6 (including Marigold Medical)	1
Standards for "full" costs (11 companies)	9 (including Tulip Tyres)	2	
Totals	11	8	1

6.3 The contribution concept combined with actual costing

If companies employ standard costing systems, it is relatively easy to establish how the standards are compiled and how those costs are employed in financial reporting. It is not quite so easy to undertake a similar exercise where companies *do not* set standards. Nevertheless, checking the manner in which these companies valued stock was helpful in reassuring the researchers that their product costing methods were, indeed, consistent with a contribution/marginal costing orientation. Table 6.3 summarises the methods used.

Shasta Ships is engaged in the maintenance and repair of ships so that it is not in mainstream manufacturing. At this company, most stock is either contract-specific or materials in nature (valued at replacement cost). Sunflower Seals, similarly, manufactures product (seals for marine engineering) to customer specification and values stock at actual cost on a last-in-first-out basis. Both Shasta Ships and Sunflower Seals aim to value the cost of contracts/production at as close to actual cost as possible.

Cornflower Coated Steels and Tiger-flower Tinplate are primarily steel wholesalers although Tiger-flower Tinplate also has steel preparation activities. These companies value stock at (actual) material cost. The division of Oak Oils studied is also largely a "wholesaler", purchasing its product from "upstream" refineries at standard direct cost and continuing to value product on this basis in its internal reporting. And Campion Catalysts is also an intermediary, purchasing product from manufacturing operations in Belgium, Luxembourg and the USA.

Two companies, Bluebell Building Products and Carnation Cans, are owned by multinationals based in Belgium and France respectively and have similar internal reporting formats. In both companies, depreciation (including manufacturing depreciation) appears near the foot of the P&L, below administration and marketing expenses. Neither company includes all manufacturing overhead in stock and Bluebell Building Products has, until recently, valued stock at material and direct labour cost only. This has been accepted by auditors in the past ("I have never been in a company where they've made an adjustment.") but, in 2002, this was

Table 6.3: Practices in companies that employ the contribution concept but not standard costing systems (eight companies)

Company	Basis of stock valuation	Comment
Shasta Ships	Materials at replacement cost	Auditors have accepted this practice because the value involved is not material. There are overhead recovery rates (for use in estimating) but overhead is written off as a period cost.
Sunflower Seals	Materials on last-in-first-out basis	Overhead rates are set so that margins on products can be assessed but they are not used to absorb overhead into stock. This is acceptable because stocks carried are not judged material.
Cornflower Coated Steels	Materials at actual cost or net realisable value	Materials represent the largest asset in this wholesaling business.
Tiger-flower Tinplate	Materials at actual cost	Auditors accept the valuation of materials at actual cost in this wholesaling business.
Oak Oils	Materials at actual (transfer) cost	An "intermediary", valuing materials received at transfer price paid and writing off overhead as a period cost.
Campion Catalysts	Materials at actual (transfer) cost	Another intermediary, valuing stock at transfer price (which includes variances incurred in the manufacturing operations).
Bluebell Building Products	Materials and direct labour cost only, but recently some overhead has been included in the value of stock	The anticipated introduction of international standards has led to the inclusion of manufacturing overhead in the value of stock.
Carnation Cans	Material, labour and some (but not all) manufacturing overhead	Auditors appear to have been a little unhappy with stock valuation procedures and the introduction of standard costs might help to resolve this.

changed by including an overhead adjustment to the value of work-in-progress and finished goods. Asked whether this would make a big difference our interviewee responded: "The audit manager . . . said to me that won't really affect you because there's not a lot of difference between the UK and IAS standards. Well I'm afraid he's in for a bit of a shock when he sees some of the adjustments." This is, of course, because, although the UK and IAS standards are similar, the introduction of IAS has been used to trigger a significant change in accounting practice.

Carnation Cans values stock at material, labour and manufacturing overhead cost but this does not include manufacturing depreciation. Again auditors have accepted this practice. "One of the comments they always make is 'well it would be nice to have an activity-based costing or some form of costing system' and we've kind of strung them along on the activity-based costing one for a while thinking oh that's coming in so next year will be fine."

Analysis of the stock valuation methods used in these 8 companies shows that they are consistent with marginal costing methods. The first 6 companies are either contractors or wholesalers and, for these companies, excluding overhead from the value of stock seems sensible. The remaining companies, Bluebell Building Products and Carnation Cans, are conventional manufacturers but, in these two companies, the costing systems are changing. There is interest in the inclusion of overhead in stock values and, at Carnation Cans, in the introduction of ABC and/or standard costing.

6.4 The gross profit/margin concept combined with standard costing

We now turn to those companies that emphasise the reporting of gross profit or gross margin (rather than contribution margin). In this section we review the methods employed by those companies that combine this emphasis with standard costing systems. Seven companies fall into this category. Table 6.4 summarises the use of standards and variance analysis by these companies.

All of these companies set standards for materials, labour and overhead and they also report variances for all these elements of cost. Variance analysis in these companies does seem to be more extensive and, generally, a more serious undertaking than in the companies discussed in previous sections.

At Holly Health Furniture our interviewee commented: ". . . we do calculate all the variances and we do use them." At this

Table 6.4: Standard costs in companies that report gross profit or gross margin and do not employ the contribution concept in financial reporting (seven companies)

Company	Standards set	Variances calculated	Comment
Holly Health Furniture	Material, Labour, Overhead	Material, Labour, Overhead	Price, usage/efficiency and overhead recovery variances
Shamrock Shelving	Material, Labour, Overhead	Material, Labour, Overhead	"Full set" of materials, labour and overhead variances. Explicit separation of variable overhead planned.
Willow Windows	Material, Labour, Overhead	Material, Labour, Overhead	Material variances in some detail. Labour and overhead incurred reported, together with labour and overhead recovered.
Robin Rectifiers	Material, Labour, Overhead	Material, Labour, Overhead	Standard cost, standard margin and associated variances reported – complying with the US GAAP
Apricot Aeros	Material, Labour, Overhead	Material, Labour, Overhead	Labour and overhead recovered for each manufacturing cell (about 370 in total)
Apple Aeros	Material, Labour, Overhead	Material, Labour, Overhead	Overhead recovered for each cell. Variances calculated but material price and labour efficiency receive most attention.
Daisy Drinks	Material, Labour, Overhead	Material, Labour, Overhead	Manufacturing variances accounted for after striking gross margin.

company full standard costs are also used to derive transfer prices although these are used with care. For example: "Holly Health Germany might come back and say we've got a very big deal coming up here, we need help with our profits etc." In a case like this the implication is that the "normal" transfer price would be discounted.

At Shamrock Shelving, standards are set for material, labour and overhead and more sophistication is planned with the separate identification of standards for variable overhead. Like Holly Health Furniture, this company also employs full standard costs as the basis for setting internal transfer prices.

Willow Windows is also serious about the use of standard costs and variances. Although the presentation of labour and overhead spent and recovered in the P&L is simple, there is a separate, very detailed, analysis of labour variances and material variances that are divided into price and usage components. This company also uses its full product costs in order to set transfer prices and, in a sense, has manipulated these by not changing overhead recovery rates even though volume have grown. This could mean the loss of business if selling companies based their tenders on overestimated costs but our interviewee was well aware of this danger and would permit sales at below transfer price if, otherwise, good business would be lost.

Robin Rectifiers adopts a global policy in relation to standard setting and sets "global standards" for its products at headquarters in the USA. Our interviewee was unable to provide a detailed account of the methods employed but it is clear that the systems are sophisticated. In addition to the "global standards", local product cost standards are set and it is clear that variance analysis could become complex. In an international group, exchange rate movements can be very important and material price variances are divided into that element caused by exchange rate movements and the residual "real" price variance.

Both Apricot Aeros and Apple Aeros are suppliers to the aerospace industry. These are large companies employ sophisticated approaches to standard costing with standards for materials and labour and standard recovery rates for their many manufacturing cells. Both these companies are suppliers to the Ministry of Defence and full-manufacturing costs might be important in justifying prices charged to this important customer.

Finally, Daisy Drinks is another large company, now under American ownership, that takes standard costing and variance reporting seriously. Like Robin Rectifiers, material price variance due to exchange rate movements is calculated and this company analyses material usage variances identifying mix variances versus standard product recipes.

Overall, these companies, emphasising gross profit or gross margin in their P&L reporting, employ standard costing systems that include standard recovery rates for manufacturing overhead. The "full" manufacturing costs are employed in the calculation of gross profit and variances are reported for materials, labour and overhead. All 7 of these companies set standard overhead recovery rates and calculate overhead variances (although, as noted earlier, none analyse the overhead volume variance into capacity and efficiency components).

On balance, these companies tend to be larger[22] than the companies discussed in previous sections and the use of standard costing seems to be more formalised and institutionalised. There are examples of companies using full manufacturing costs as a basis for transfer pricing and the availability of full costs is convenient in the two aerospace suppliers where prices have to be justified to major customers.

6.5 The gross profit/margin concept combined with actual costing

We identify only two companies in this category, Esther Enzymes and Acacia Aerokit. Both these companies are major contractors and both book materials at actual cost to contracts or works orders. Both also book labour costs to contracts and attribute overhead to contracts using recovery rates. At Esther Enzymes, overhead is recovered against the time assigned for each project. This company specialises in drug discovery involving major projects with "recovery" of labour and overhead costs into contract accounts. Revenue recognition and cash collection (against part completed contracts) are major issues for this company. At Acacia Aerokit, two "burden rates"[23] are used, one based on materials and one based on labour hours in order to absorb overhead into

---

[22]We confess that this is a rather subjective assessment of "larger". Companies can have high turnover but (like Daisy Drinks) this might be inflated by duty or the high turnover might be deceptive because relatively few employees are needed to generate it. Nevertheless, our knowledge of these companies does indicate that, in addition to having significant business unit turnover, they also tend to be part of large international groups.

[23]Acacia Aerokit is a subsidiary of an American multinational and employs American terminology, hence "burden" instead of "overhead" recovery rates.

contract values. The very significant amount of stock at the latter company means that great care is taken in its valuation and recovery rates are checked month to month and adjustments can be made to the value of stock if they are deemed necessary.

Neither of these companies is considered to employ standard costing systems but both set overhead recovery rates and ensure that the value of their (very significant) work-in-progress includes manufacturing overhead. The methods employed to value stock are consistent with their classification as companies that place the main emphasis on gross margin (not contribution margin) reporting.

6.6 Companies not easily classified as primarily contribution or gross margin oriented

We turn, finally, to four companies, Daffodil Dairy, Larkspur Lighting, Thyme Tanneries and Iris Instruments, that proved difficult to classify as primarily "contribution-oriented" or "gross profit-oriented".

The first company, Daffodil Dairy, probably adopts the simplest approach to accounting. The presentation of its P&L implies a fairly straightforward closure of its financial books of account. This company does not employ a sophisticated approach to costing and our interviewee simply referred to the inclusion of some overhead in the value of stock if stocks became significant. Although Daffodil Dairy does not refer to contribution in its reporting it does write overhead off as a period cost and it is this practice that makes the company difficult to classify.

Larkspur Lighting also adopts a very simple approach to costing and our interviewee was rather dissatisfied with: "... one of the lowest levels of accounting that I've ever done to be honest." He went on to say that: "... materials are based on actual and ... we don't include any labour in our products at the moment. We've never done any timings or anything ... so it's really, really basic." Like Daffodil Dairy, there is no reference to contribution in this company's P&L. However, there is no doubt that marginal cost principles are employed because the (small) stockholding is valued at material cost only. Our interviewee explained that, for external reporting "We just put that stock is valued at cost, if anyone asks what that is then we haven't lied. . . ." Our interviewee would prefer to include manufacturing overhead in the value of stock: "I would like to, there was everywhere else I've worked in manufacturing." However, one of the constraining factors is the attitude of the managing director (who owns the company). He is concerned that the inclusion of labour cost might "fake the value of stock". It seems that the situation at Larkspur Lighting echoes that Elm Engineering where the managing director took the view that the safest method of accounting for labour was to "write it all off".

The third company is Thyme Tanneries, a company that has employed relatively sophisticated absorption production costs. However, this company has switched to presenting financial information by simply closing its financial books of account and this has obviated the need for reconciliation of the financial and cost accounting profits. Although contribution is not mentioned in the P&L format the layout identifies variable and fixed works overhead separately and fixed overhead is written off as a period cost. Our interviewee confirmed that prices were increasingly market-driven and, despite the continued use of "full" costs, contribution analysis had become more important.

The fourth company in this section is Iris Instruments, one of the early "pilot" companies visited. This company is difficult to classify because it includes a "material gross profit" line in its P&L and can thus be deemed to employ contribution concepts. Labour and overhead appear at actual cost in the P&L and, as labour/overhead recovery rates are also set, adjustments are undertaken to account for under- or over-recovery of labour and overhead in the P&L. We were unable to properly understand how these adjustments were performed and this is the reason that the company appears as "difficult to classify".

6.7 Conclusions: Margins, variances, costing systems and "Relevance Lost"

Despite some difficulties of interpretation and understanding a coherent picture of practice in the 41 survey companies emerges from this and the last two chapters.

In Chapter 4 we identified 28 companies that could reasonably be judged to employ the contribution concept in their internal financial reporting and, additionally, a further 4 companies might be added to this group if a more liberal view of "contribution concepts" were adopted. Thus, at least 68% of the survey companies might be employing contribution methods.

There were two major caveats attached to our analysis in Chapter 4. The first was that some subjectivity was involved in the analysis because of the terminology employed in a number of companies. In particular, several companies that were judged to employ contribution concepts used financial reporting terminology, especially references to "gross profit" and "gross margin", in their P&L reporting. The second caveat related to the number of companies that, while adopting a contribution style layout, also include an adjustment in their P&L that ensures that net profit is reported on a "full absorption" basis.

In Chapter 5 we identified 30 survey companies that employ standard costs. Thus, almost 75% of survey companies employ standards and, where standards are not employed, in eight companies, this is understandable because of the nature of their business as contractors or "wholesale" intermediaries.

The major caveat in Chapter 5 was that, although most of the survey companies demonstrably set standards, this does not mean that they use them extensively. Many companies do not set standard recovery rates for overhead and, of those that do, some use their "full standard costs" only as a means of placing a value on the content of overhead in stocks.

In this chapter we have attempted to analyse the interaction between approaches to financial reporting and the costing systems adopted in survey companies.

In the 28 "contribution companies" their marginal costing orientation was confirmed with the 20 companies that set standards concentrating on material, labour and variable overhead variances.

Although contribution companies concentrated on variable cost variances, 11 of them combined their contribution orientation with "full" standard costs and set standard overhead recovery rates. Here financial reporting and costing systems seem "loosely coupled" with full standard costs being used to make a P&L adjustment so that net profit can be reported on a fully absorbed basis. Eight of these companies use their full standard costs to make a P&L adjustment so that *monthly* net profit is reported on a "fully absorbed" basis. One company reports monthly net profit on *both* marginal and fully absorbed bases. And two companies report monthly net profit on a marginal basis, adjusting this annually for financial reporting purposes. In the 9 companies that do not set overhead recovery rates there is a greater tendency to make the "full absorption stock and profit adjustment" annually and one of these companies bases its *external* financial reporting on stocks valued at variable cost.

There are 8 "contribution companies" that do not employ standards and analysis of their approaches to valuing stock confirmed their interest in contribution ideas and marginal costing methods. The methods used in contractors and "wholesalers" are understandable and, in the two more conventional manufacturers, there is increased interest in costing systems and the inclusion of overhead in the value of stock. In one of these companies, until recently, the value of stock had included only material and labour cost.

We conclude that most of the survey companies employ contribution ideas in their internal financial reporting. Although some set overhead recovery rates, these are typically employed only for establishing the value of overhead carried in stock. The number of companies adopting contribution ideas surprised us because we had anticipated that most companies would adopt absorption costing methods and we had presumed these policies to be mutually exclusive. This survey shows that financial reporting and costing systems may be "loosely coupled" and some companies might employ contribution reporting formats *and* fully absorbed costs.

The "relevance lost" thesis of cost accounting rests on a chain of reasoning that presumes that financial reporting regulations dominate internal financial reporting by predisposing companies to the use of absorption costs. These costs, designed only to meet the requirements of financial regulation, are unlikely to provide a good basis for management decisions and thus cost accounting loses its relevance. Our finding that companies employ contribution methods and concentrate on marginal costs and variances seemed to refute the relevance lost thesis. Marginal costing methods are not acceptable for external financial reporting so it seemed that companies were *not* dominated by externally imposed regulations in their internal procedures. Additionally, if absorbed costs are used *only* as a means of valuing stock then there is little evidence that these full costs are being misused. However, we reconsidered this initial conclusion on realising that several of these companies make *monthly* adjustments so that internally reported net profit is consistent with financial reporting requirements. In *this* respect it is possible to discern the influence of financial regulation in internal practices.

The minority of companies that have an obviously gross profit or gross margin (as opposed to contribution) orientation typically employ standard costing systems and always employ overhead recovery rates in order to "absorb" overhead into stock and cost of sales. The costing systems employed in these, typically larger, often multinational, companies are consistent with their "gross profit orientation". Internal financial reporting is more obviously institutionalised and formalised in these companies and they are much more likely to at least calculate (if not use) overhead recovery variances. These companies also seem more likely to use their full standard costs as a basis for setting transfer prices and, in major defence suppliers, the availability of full costs is no doubt useful in justifying prices charged.

Our analysis so far has led us to the conclusion that many of the companies in this survey prefer contribution style presentations because of their simplicity and utility in providing managerial information. Often there is loose coupling between reporting formats and costing systems with the latter simply providing the means to value stock and ensure that reported net profit complies with the requirements of financial reporting. In the minority of companies that employ full absorption costing systems and gross profit reporting there may be more evidence of "financial reporting dominance". This debate turns on the treatment of manufacturing overhead in the survey companies, the issue addressed in Chapter 7.

The Treatment of Overhead Costs

7.1 Introduction

The treatment and analysis of overhead cost has been a key thread in the discussions of the last three chapters. The location of manufacturing overhead, above or below the gross or contribution margin line, was important in determining how companies prefer to present information to managers. The interest (or rather lack of it) in overhead recovery and overhead variances was seen as further confirmation that many survey companies prefer contribution analysis.

At first these results appeared to refute the "relevance lost" thesis that presumed the domination of externally mandated absorption costing. However, a number of "contribution companies" include an adjustment in their P&L so that net profit is reported in accordance with absorption costing principles. In this respect a number of companies *do* seem to be influenced by external reporting requirements.

We begin this chapter (Sections 7.2 and 7.3) by summarising the practices of survey companies in their P&L treatment of overhead. Section 7.2 recaps some of the discussion of the last three chapters, summarising the practices of "contribution companies" in writing off or holding manufacturing overhead in stock. We conclude this section with some suggestions for *accounting* for overhead in companies that favour contribution presentations. In Section 7.3 we turn to the accounting treatment of overhead in those companies that favour gross profit or gross margin accounting. These companies employ the volume-based overhead absorption rates that one might expect. We conclude that, in these companies, costing systems are more "tightly coupled" with financial reporting than in the contribution-oriented companies. There is greater potential for the "inappropriate" use of product costs in these companies but we could see little evidence of it in the survey companies.

One of the textbook advantages of marginal costing methods is the ability to unambiguously attribute expenses to "cost objects". At its simplest, this means tracing variable (manufacturing) costs to individual products or product groups and establishing contribution for individual products or product groups. A number of companies explicitly perform such analyses and several companies go further, attributing overhead to product groups, business units or market segments in order to gain insights into the performance of aspects of the business. We report the extent of these practices in the survey companies in Section 7.4.

Tracing costs to product units and then to business segments is in the spirit of the activity-based "cost hierarchy" that sees costs in terms of unit-related, batch-related and facility-sustaining "tiers". The analyses described in Section 7.4 have a certain affinity with what Jones and Dugdale (2001) termed "second wave", contribution-oriented ABC. The "first wave" of ABC aimed to develop "more accurate" unit absorption costs and this form of ABC is probably more familiar in textbooks and, for students, in examinations. We analyse the extent of this "first wave" ABC in Section 7.5. No survey companies adopt "first wave" ABC although some companies have experimented with the technique and some are currently interested in it. Nevertheless, we conclude that few survey companies see ABC as a crucial development in their costing or financial reporting.

The final section, 7.6, includes some reflections on the costing and reporting systems chosen in the survey companies and we conclude that these are driven by a number of factors: nature of business, ownership, history, decision usefulness, conservatism, introduction of perceived "best practice", financial regulation, etc.

7.2 Treatment of manufacturing overhead in internal financial reporting by companies employing contribution concepts

It will be recalled that, with some difficulty concerning terminology, 28 companies were eventually judged to be employing contribution concepts and a further 4 companies were difficult to classify but seemed to employ some aspects of the contribution approach. We begin by summarising the treatment of manufacturing overhead in these 32 companies.

Given that manufacturing overhead should be included in the value of stock for external financial reporting, this can be a major issue in these companies and we have seen that the methods adopted can vary significantly:

♦ Some companies make no adjustments at all, simply reporting the value of stock on a marginal cost basis both in their monthly accounts and in their annual financial reports.
♦ Some companies adjust stock for the value of manufacturing overhead but do this only annually. In these companies, monthly net profit is reported on a marginal cost basis.
♦ Some companies adjust the value of stock for the value of manufacturing overhead and do this on a monthly basis. In these companies, although a contribution style format is adopted and, typically, sales are matched with some variant of variable costs, net profit is reported on an absorption cost basis.
♦ One company reports net profit on *both* marginal and absorption cost bases.

Companies that exclude manufacturing overhead from the value of stock (10 companies)

The companies in this group comprise Shasta Ships, Sunflower Seals, Tiger-flower Tinplate, Oak Oil, Cornflower Coated Steel, Campion Catalysts, Daffodil Dairy, Pine Packaging, Peony Prosthetics and Larkspur Lighting.

The first six of these are contractors and intermediaries. The contractors recognise revenue as major contracts are completed and write off overhead as a period cost against this revenue. The wholesalers/intermediaries add little manufacturing content to the product and so this value can be ignored in valuing stock. Daffodil Dairies adopts a traditional approach to financial accounting and includes overhead in the value of its stock (mainly milk) only if it is significant. Pine Packaging has little need for stock value adjustments because revenue is recognised on completion of production.

Peony Prosthetics and Larkspur Lighting are fairly conventional manufacturing companies so the omission of overhead in their stock values is more surprising. At Peony Prosthetics the exclusion of overhead is, to some extent, a continuation of historic practice. At Larkspur Lighting the practice owes something to the owner's/managing director's conservatism (his desire not to "fake" the value of stock) and to the relatively low (immaterial) values of stock carried.

Companies that include part of the value of manufacturing overhead in stock (1 company)

Carnation Cans is rather difficult to classify because, following the format of its (Gallic influenced) P&L this company includes some manufacturing overhead in the value of stock but excludes manufacturing depreciation in this calculation.

Companies that make annual adjustments for the value of overhead in stock (9 companies)

The companies in this group are Flying Foods, Aster Autovending, Marigold Medical, Bluebell Building Products, Elm Engineering, Petunia Plastics, Fir Films, Flax Fans and Poppy Plasterboard.

These companies are conscious of the need to make an adjustment to their accounts in order to comply with financial reporting requirements but only do this on an annual basis (or rather, in the case of Marigold Medical, infrequently). These companies therefore report their internal, month-to-month financial results on a marginal costing basis.

Companies that make monthly adjustments for the value of overhead in stock (11 companies)

The companies in this group are Cherry Components, Everlasting Extinguishers, Tiger-lily Typing, Fuschia Fabrics, Forget-me-not Foam, Primrose Plastics, Rose Resins, Honesty Hydraulics, Heather Health Equipment, Iris Instruments and Thyme Tanneries.

These companies generally adopt contribution style reporting formats so that, typically, manufacturing variable costs are matched with sales. *However*, an adjustment is made (usually via a one line "movement of manufacturing overhead in stock" journal entry) in the monthly accounts so that reported net profit is consistent with absorption costing methods. Despite their interest in contribution reporting these companies are influenced by external reporting requirements in their internal monthly financial reporting.

Companies that report both monthly marginal costing and absorption costing net profit (1 company)

Just one company, Tulip Tyres, reports net profit according to marginal costing principles but then makes the "overhead in stock" adjustment so that net profit is also reported on an absorption costing basis. As has been described previously, Tulip Tyres is one company that has reviewed its reporting methods carefully in the recent past and concluded that marginal cost–oriented reporting is most consistent with its information needs. The presentation now adopted:

Sales

(Variable costs)

Contribution

(Fixed costs)

Operating profit/(loss) before whole cost adjustment

Whole cost adjustment

Operating profit/(loss)

Comment

In reaching this conclusion Tulip Tyres reminds us of the advice given by Solomons (1965: 111):

> As we have seen, some of the arguments for and against direct costing are evenly balanced. Some of the arguments for it are very strong, particularly the ease with which certain decisions, superimposed on past results, can be projected into the future to give the probable results of those decisions. The real objections of auditors to its use for financial reporting reinforce the conclusion to be drawn that a combination method which gives the best of both worlds has much to commend it. This is the way that direct costing is coming to be used, and the way in which its use is likely to spread.
>
> The combination method requires that, after the profit for the period has been ascertained by direct methods, an adjustment for period cost be made in the divisional income statement to the book value of inventory. It is unnecessary to make a detailed allocation of actual period costs to products for the

purpose of this adjustment. All that is required for the determination of profit is to calculate what proportion of the period expense in total is applicable to the change in inventory which occurred during the period.

Although Solomons was British, his seminal work on divisional performance measurement was based on practices in the USA where the influence of financial regulation over stock valuation and profit reporting took hold earlier than in the UK. As Dugdale and Jones (2003) observe, the inclusion of manufacturing overhead in the value of stock was not mandated in the UK until the issue of SSAP9 in 1975. However, by the last quarter of the twentieth century, financial reporting practice in the US and the UK had been harmonised and Solomons' comments became relevant on both sides of the Atlantic. His suggestion is perhaps even more relevant today because, with further harmonisation based on international accounting standards, more companies across the world will face the issue of reconciling their preferred internal reporting system with external reporting requirements.

Recommendations

"Contribution companies" might be advised in different ways according to their information and policy requirements.

First, there are those companies that effectively report contribution and gross margin because they are, to all intents and purposes, the same thing. Wholesalers and intermediaries fall into this category. In relation to manufacturing overhead these companies face only minor stock valuation problems because little manufacturing value is added.

Second, there are companies that hold very little stock, either because of their JIT policies or their approaches to revenue recognition. In these companies, stock may be accepted as immaterial and a marginal or variable cost valuation might be accepted even for external reporting.

Third, there are companies that wish to adopt a marginal cost presentation for internal purposes but need to make an adjustment to profit in order to comply with external reporting prerogatives. For these companies Solomons' advice holds good today. A simple, aggregate adjustment could be made either annually or monthly.

Fourth, there are those companies that wish to expense manufacturing overhead periodically, but, in addition, have an interest in fully absorbed product costs, perhaps for estimating, pricing or transfer pricing. In these companies it might make sense to use the "full" product costs in order to make the "overhead in stock" adjustment. These companies might adopt the approach adopted by Tulip Tyres. Given the availability of full manufacturing costs in these companies, it seems natural to use these costs in making the "overhead in stock adjustment". Following the example of Tulip Tyres the adjustment can be calculated every month so that any divergence between marginal net profit and absorption net profit is identified. It would not be wise to approach the end of the financial year without realising that the "absorption cost adjustment" is about to mean a large and unexpected debit to the P&L account!

In sum, we suggest that companies that favour a contribution approach make an adjustment to net profit so that "absorption net profit" is also reported. Calculation of the adjustment might be based on full product costs and, like Tulip Tyres, a full standard costing system might be employed in order to establish the monthly adjustment. However, this is not necessary, and as Solomons showed almost 40 years ago, a relatively simple calculation can be employed in order to establish the adjustment needed.

7.3 Treatment of manufacturing overhead in internal financial reporting by companies employing gross profit concepts

There are 9 survey companies that seem to show no interest in contribution style reporting and most (7) of these employ standard costing systems that include standard overhead recovery rates. In the two companies that specialise in contract work (Acacia Aerokit and Esther Enzymes), where standard costing is not really appropriate, "standard" overhead recovery rates are still employed so that labour and overhead are charged to contracts and/or works orders. In these 9 companies, issues concerning the inclusion of overhead in stock hardly arise because stock is valued at full manufactured cost as a matter of policy.[24]

The "gross profit" companies employ traditional approaches to standard setting and overhead recovery. Although there can be many rates (as many as 370 at Apple Aeros), the number of different recovery bases is limited.

♦ At Holly Health Furniture, overhead is recovered against standard labour hours using a "rather old" MRP system. Group would like to see this replaced but, as it works, the system is understood and the company profitable the company has been given dispensation to continue to use it.

♦ At Shamrock Shelving again, a rather old MRP system is in operation and, again, Group would like to see it replaced. Our interviewee was dissatisfied with the system because there were some 30 process hour-based rates but actual costs were collected inconsistently in only seven cost centres. This was to be addressed by the use of 16 process hour-based rates and the consistent collection of actual costs. (Other improvements planned were the separate analysis of labour, variable overhead and fixed overhead.)

♦ At Willow Windows, overhead is absorbed per unit manufactured but the rates are four years out of date having been set when output was significantly less than now. This is a conscious decision to ensure that transfer prices between group companies are not understated.

♦ At Esther Enzymes, an integrated MRP system is employed but, although the project accounting modules are used: ". . . what we are not doing is a bill of materials." At this contracting company, overhead is recovered according to time allocated to each project using standard rates for each individual. There is under- or over-recovery of overhead depending on whether overhead "recovered" is greater or less than actual expenditure.

---

[24]In principle an adjustment can be necessary in companies that value stock at standard cost if the standards are judged not to be a close approximation to actual cost. This issue did not seem to arise in the survey companies, although this might be because at Willow Windows (where standards are set high to ensure that transfer prices are not understated) this is because relatively low stocks are carried.

◆ At Robin Rectifiers, standard costing is adopted as policy across the group and overhead is recovered on units produced in the fabrication process (which involves expensive equipment and heavy depreciation charges) and on labour and process hours in the assembly processes.

◆ At Acacia Aerokit, two burden rates are used, based on material value and labour hours to absorb overhead into works orders. As the size of inventory could be £7–9 million this issue exercised our interviewee. He was concerned that when works orders were closed ". . . if things don't hook up properly . . . you can be left with sort of hanging debits which should really be expense." In this company, if standard recovery rates drift out of line with actual rates, adjustments are made on a monthly basis. "You only need 1% of that [stock value] to change and it could be getting up towards £100,000 and obviously we don't want shocks like that at the year end."

◆ At Apricot Aeros a large number of overhead recovery rates are set, one for each manufacturing cell, based on standard process hours.

◆ At Apple Aeros, again multiple rates are set, one for each manufacturing cell. At this company the rates are almost invariably based on labour hours although, for the "burn-in" cabinets the overhead rates are based on process hours.

◆ At the process manufacturer, Daisy Drinks, labour costs are subsumed within overhead and this is recovered per litre of product (with separate rates for each product line) and, for packaging costs, per unit of sale (boxes, cartons, etc.) with a separate rate for each packaging line. In an echo of other companies, our interviewee referred to a "very old" MRP system that ought to be replaced within the next two to three years. The American parent wished to standardise on a new ERP system across the company.

Consideration of the detailed approaches to overhead recovery in these companies confirms their interest in and commitment to generating full manufactured costs for individual products. In these companies it is usual to establish standard cost of sales and related variances. Even in the large scale contracting companies where actual material costs are booked to contracts and works orders there is under- or over-recovery of labour and overhead using standard overhead recovery rates.

The methods used in these companies are traditional "textbook" approaches and there is a theoretical possibility that the product costs generated might mislead managers as to the "true" profitability of individual products. However, in two respects these companies are more sophisticated than the "relevance lost" companies that formed the basis of case studies in the 1980s. Although labour overhead recovery rates are common in these companies they also use other rates based on materials, process hours and units. And there is little evidence of plant wide, "blanket" overhead recovery rates. These companies generally seem prepared to set as many rates as they deem useful and/or necessary. The use of multiple recovery rates and bases does not, of course, guarantee that product costs do not mislead but this was not an obvious problem to our interviewees.

7.4 The analysis of overhead for responsibility, product or segmental reporting

A pilot study finding that surprised one of the researchers was what appeared to be the innovative use of contribution reporting combined with the measurement of business units by deducting *attributable* overhead from contribution. We reported findings in the initial, pilot, companies in Chapter 3. Three of these, Fuschia Fabrics, Flying Foods and Flax Fans adopt similar reporting formats based on contribution reporting and go on to report the performance of separate market-focused business units after deducting attributable (selling) overheads.

These presentations seemed eminently sensible both for decision-making (where contribution per unit or product group could readily be ascertained) and for responsibility accounting (if the reporting segments were aligned with organisational responsibilities). Our speculation was that manufacturing companies might be "relegating" manufacturing overhead to the foot of the P&L and concentrating, instead, on generating sufficient contribution from their market-oriented selling organisations. The next sections analyse the extent to which contribution companies extend their basic marginal cost formats so as to establish the "contribution" generated at different organisational levels.

"Contribution companies" that seem to employ relatively unsophisticated analysis (9 companies)

A number of companies do not appear to employ very sophisticated approaches to cost analysis.

This is understandable at Elm Engineering where turnover of approximately £1.5 million per year hardly justifies sophisticated analysis. Marigold Medical, also relatively small with turnover of about £7 million per annum, limits its P&L analysis to separating UK and export sales. And Aster Autovending (£11 million per annum) employs a similar analysis, splitting sales by product and (one) major customer. Fir Films, with turnover of about £15 million per annum, also has little analysis. At this company, where individual products sell for several thousand pounds, there is some geographical analysis but: "We're fairly low volume and we don't see a huge value in breaking it out by product."

Larkspur Lighting is larger in turnover terms (about £25 million per annum) but, as we have noted before, employs simple systems. It seems that control over profit margins is exercised when orders are accepted. Sales people are expected to make at least 50% on: ". . . everything [cost] they see on the screen." Systems might creak in this company but product is delivered on time with low stocks and with tight control over product profitability.

The remaining four companies in this section are undergoing or have recently undergone systems or organisational change. The two "Gallic" companies, Carnation Cans and Bluebell Building Products, are attempting to improve their reporting systems. At Carnation Cans, a SAP system has been installed and our interviewee is interested in standard costing while Group pushes its ABC initiative. Bluebell Building Products operates two divisions with separate manufacturing plants concentrating on windows and building products (such as fascia boards) but relatively unsophisticated systems mean that there has been no attempt, until recently using spreadsheet methods, to apportion overhead to the two divisions.

Two more companies, Peony Prosthetics and Heather Health Equipment, seem to be undergoing organisational change. At Peony Prosthetics two divisions were created ". . . to preserve an illusion to the National Health Service that we provided an independent service and that the clinicians that work for us had the freedom to provide, or rather prescribe anyone's products." This strategy had not worked and the separate reporting formats created by the two divisions were to be re-merged. And Heather Health Equipment had adopted more complex systems in the past with "...all sorts of nice variances." However, takeover by a large (UK) group has switched attention to "...actuals, not how you got there." Our interviewee was interested in ABC but, given the new parent company, the climate was not right for its introduction.

Companies that emphasise product line and other variants of contribution (19 companies)

One of the advantages of contribution approaches is the unequivocal attribution of variable cost to product units and the relative ease with which contribution can be calculated by product group. There were specific references to this sort of analysis at a number of companies. Everlasting Extinguishers analyse "product range profitability" based on the contributions reported in the P&L. This is quite sophisticated in that variances are "added back" for each product so that *actual* profitability can be estimated. Cornflower Coated Steel analyses "gross margin" (contribution) by product, customer and region. Thyme Tanneries now employs a relatively simple approach to management accounting but identifies sales and material costs by each separate product group. And Daffodil Dairy analyses sales and cost of sales (largely material costs) for each product (bottled, doorstep, franchisee, etc.) and by sales channel.

Some companies are more obviously *organised* on product group lines and, here again, contribution formats make it easy to analyse "product group contribution performance". Primrose Plastics has three main product groups (building products, gas/water pipes and large systems) and contribution margin can be attributed to each product group. Tiger-flower Tinplate has two product lines, selling bulk tinplate on the one hand and processing capacity on the other. The two lines of business are relatively independent and their performance can be reported separately. For reporting convenience, the same format is used for both businesses and despite differences in terminology, contribution margin is important in both businesses. Forget-me-not Foam has two major product ranges for household furniture and the automotive (soundproofing) market. These two market segments are obviously dissimilar and one might expect them to be reported separately. However, the same processes are employed for both product ranges and our interviewee noted that ". . . it's quite tricky to separate them out." He added: "I have to say however that it is something that is possible that we will be doing in the future."

It is, of course, possible to go further, after establishing contribution by product group, overhead can be allocated to product groups and a number of companies allocate their *manufacturing* overhead. At Poppy Plasterboard our interviewee mentioned the extension of contribution analysis to establish "industrial result" by product group. At Cherry Components, "direct profit" is established for each product group, then follows allocation of overhead to products ". . . right down to net profit". Tiger-lily Typing reports for its traditional product range and, separately, for its new product range, allocating manufacturing overhead to each. Petunia Plastics had three divisions (plastic products for the building industry, wiring systems and power components) but merged these in order to integrate its product offering. However, internally, separate reporting continues ". . . that goes down to gross profit for the old divisions." Iris Instruments adopted an analysis of sales and contribution into the UK and "rest of world". However, since 1999, a business unit approach has been adopted with overhead attributed to business units according to the standard costs of the products they produce (overhead recovery rates for labour and overhead set for each manufacturing cell).

A key issue is the meaningfulness (or meaninglessness) of this analysis. Textbooks and the management accounting literature are replete with examples of the foolhardiness of apportioning "fixed" overhead that will be unaffected by decisions affecting particular business segments.[25] Our interviewees were well aware of the issues involved. At Poppy Plasterboard the apportionment of non-manufacturing costs, including selling and marketing costs, is considered to be too artificial to be worth pursuing. At Cherry Components our interviewee felt that reporting net profit by

---

[25]The "Farmer Brown" example from Ryan and Hobson (1985: 220) and the celebrated "Peanut vendor" case (Wilson and Chua, 1988: 391) come to mind as instructive and humorous examples.

product group was: ". . . a lot of that is nonsense but it's a group convention. . .". He then went on to provide one of the classic rationales for the practice: ". . . To be fair to them they are all well aware of the limitations of it but they want to make people aware that you've got to be responsible all the way down." And concluded: "It's open to a lot of manipulation because in groups you get more manipulation than in parliament." An example of this kind of "manipulation" is provided by Tiger-lily Typing where marketing and distribution costs are not easy to attribute to the "old" and "new" product lines. Until recently, these costs have been allocated to the traditional business (thus favouring the new product range).

We now turn to those companies that tend not to allocate or apportion manufacturing costs (unless there is a clear reason for this) but do allocate *sales, marketing and distribution* costs to product groups or business units. In the two intermediaries, Oak Oils and Campion Catalysts, this practice is hardly surprising because there is very little manufacturing cost in these companies. They purchase product from other group companies (at transfer price) and their main business is selling and marketing. Oak Oils analyses sales and gross margin (sales less the purchase cost of the product) by product group (lubricants, fuels, services) and undertakes a "sub-analysis" of fixed costs, dividing them into customer and non-customer facing categories. Campion Catalysts splits its analysis across two divisions (chemicals and oil refining) with separate analysis for the major product lines in each division. Margin for each product is easily ascertained because, in this intermediary, product is purchased from manufacturing operations in Europe and the USA. There are large sales and technical costs associated with some products and these are known by division and can be traced reasonably accurately to product lines.

The allocation of sales and marketing costs in companies that have major manufacturing operations is more surprising. Rose Resins establishes "margin on variable cost" after adding back material usage variances by product.[26] Sales expenses are apportioned to

---

[26]The practice of "adding back" variances to establish actual product group profitability has already been mentioned at Everlasting Extinguishers. At Rose Resins, each product is manufactured in a separate process so this is not difficult to arrange.

product line but the method used is not very sophisticated: ". . . just spread on volume . . . we don't tie it back to customer." At Flying Foods, contribution (referred to as gross profit) is struck after material, labour and packaging; then marketing, selling and distribution costs are attributed to each of five market segments to reveal segment contribution after marketing costs. At Fuschia Fabrics, contribution is struck after materials, labour, power, water and variable selling costs; specific conversion overhead and sales and marketing overhead is then attributed to the three marketing oriented business units. Flax Fans is divided into two customer facing divisions and, after establishing contribution (sales less materials and direct labour), marketing and selling overhead is deducted to establish "net profit" for each division. The two divisions have very different marketing philosophies and are managed separately. Tulip Tyres analyses its P&L by four business units and, separately, by eight markets. This company has set out its internal reporting in classic contribution style and sales less variable costs is established for each segment. Fixed costs are apportioned to the business units but our interviewee confirmed that the key performance for each business unit is "direct profit", defined as marginal income less *attributable* costs.

We were impressed by the practices in some companies. In particular, where a company has a "market facing" organisation it makes sense to identify the costs associated with marketing for each separate market segment. The deduction of these costs from the contribution generated by that market segment yields a meaningful calculation of "contribution after sales and marketing costs". The key to this analysis is not to apportion manufacturing costs to product groups if this does not make sense. The aim is to generate sufficient contribution (from all the "market facing" business units) to cover manufacturing and other "fixed" overhead and make a healthy return on investment.

It may not have escaped the reader's attention that three of the companies that we report as adopting these "innovative" practices were visited in the early stage of the project when the primary focus was on pricing practices. Because, in the main study, our focus was not so tightly on marketing issues as it had been in the original study it is possible that there is more interest in cost object profitability analysis than is disclosed in our data. We now suspect that the original line of questioning was more likely to elicit information about the "market facing" P&L analysis than our subsequent methodology where we asked companies to provide the format of their internal monthly P&L.

Companies that emphasise "contract profitability" (4 companies)

As might be expected, in the contracting companies, the cost object of particular concern is the contract and these companies go to some trouble to assess contract profitability. Sunflower Seals, Acacia Aerospace, Esther Enzymes and Shasta Ships, all establish order/contract profitability, using various methods of overhead recovery to achieve this. While Sunflower Seals and Shasta Ships tend towards contribution style P&Ls, and Acacia Aerospace and Esther Enzymes tend towards gross profit–oriented P&Ls, all 4 companies set overhead recovery rates and "absorb" overhead into orders/contracts. At Shasta Ships we were impressed by the obvious care that had been taken in setting three recovery rates: pence per hour on labour time (protective equipment, etc.), thousands of pounds per day per dock (establishment costs) and percentage on sales (commercial, admin, finance).

Companies that emphasise "product profitability" (1 company)

Pine Packaging has developed an interest in "job profitability" because of a more complex product mix. Standard costs (which might even include administration costs) are being developed to aid this.

Companies that adopt absorption costing systems (8 companies)

Finally we turn to those companies that adopt absorption costing systems. Without exception, in these companies, analysis of product, product group or business unit profitability begins with gross profit after "full" manufacturing cost of product. Daisy Drinks adopts a similar approach that to the "market facing" analyses referred to above. After reporting gross margin for each product group, specific marketing promotion costs are deducted to yield "gross profit" for each product group and then the apportionment of other marketing (especially advertising) costs establishes "contribution" for each product. The whole format is intended to emphasise the "brand management" orientation in the company. Perhaps Apple Aerospace has some similarities after its reorganisation ("again") into "sites" and "platforms" (platforms are market segments such as air transport, combat fixed wing aircraft, etc.). Sales and marketing costs can be attributed to platforms and therefore platform "profitability" after manufacturing and sales/marketing costs can be established. Sales and marketing costs are also apportioned to sites but only on a simple basis as a percentage of sales.

Shamrock Shelving is not quite so formal but the standard gross margin based system is supplemented, offline, by a two-dimensional analysis of gross profit: "... we have another schedule ... that is a sort of matrix, it has the sales channels across the top and the products down the side ... I can see the profits both by channel and by product." The sales force is organised by channel so channel profitability after selling costs can be easily derived.

Apricot Aeros and Robin Rectifiers are not organised on market facing lines but they do, nevertheless, undertake sophisticated analyses. Apricot Aeros employs standard absorption costing with reporting across four product groups representing different customer and market groups. Gross profit is reported for top-level product groups (engines, spares, etc.) and for the principal customer types (UK government, foreign military, etc.) Robin Rectifiers operates an absorption costing system and "above the line" there is an analysis by product family of sales, average selling price, volumes, standard cost and margin and total variance. Additionally, the company has invested heavily in a sophisticated reporting system ("... that presents itself to managers as a sales cube") that allows sales to be analysed by product, territory, customer, etc.

Finally, there are companies that emphasise the "bottom line" financial performance of their constituent divisions and employ transfer prices for sales and purchases between divisions. Willow Windows is the best example with transfer pricing between its 28 group companies organised into five divisions based on full absorption costs. The company has grown quickly over 25 years and has been publicly listed and then privatised again by its chairman. The policy of using "artificially" high transfer prices has not prevented a 60% increase in output volume over the past four years. Holly Health Furniture is now part of a vertically integrated group with a separate sales and service division: "They've kind of put vertical structures in, so they [the Swedish parent company] wanted the P&L split. That's probably the most significant change that's happened in the last while." And Honesty Hydraulics has three product divisions (hydraulic valves, lubrication systems and mechanical seals) aiming to devolve as much administrative expense to the divisions as possible. Even in a small business (turnover approximately £15 million per annum) this is seen as important. Costs that cannot be directly attributed are apportioned on the basis of turnover: ". . . as good as anything else."

7.5 Activity-based costing

None of the survey companies were actually employing ABC systems at the time of the interviews. However, some companies had experimented with the technique, some were interested in it and some had explicitly rejected it. We deal with each of these groups in turn.

Companies that had tried activity-based techniques in the past (5 companies)

Perhaps, the most convincing application of ABC was at Tiger-lily Typing where our interviewee introduced the subject by saying that "We've had some dabbles at it, yes." In fact it seems that this company had done rather more than dabbled.

> We had a big exercise about five years ago and we discovered that one of our best customers was one who was based in Israel who bought £20,000 every other month. To be honest we never saw him to be a very good customer but it turned out that they were very profitable. Then there was one customer who we thought were wonderful but what we'd forgotten or hadn't picked up was the fact that they were ordering from us twice a day, having despatches once a day. They weren't quite as good as we thought. So information like that was useful.

This information led to changes in policy so that the customer now revealed as not so good as previously assumed received deliveries only once per week.

At Heather Health Equipment our interviewee used exactly the same phrase, asked about ABC he said "We've dabbled with it." At the time of the interview, following its absorption into a larger (UK) group, this company had simplified its systems. "Everything is recovered on [labour] hours, which I disagree with, but that's the group approach, because we have activities . . . which are consuming overheads that have no labour attached to them." In this company the climate was now such that: ". . . doing anything like that at the moment would be a waste of time and effort." Nevertheless, it was clear that activity-based thinking continued to have an impact: "We do occasional ad-hoc exercises, if there's a lump of overhead we wish to reduce or something, we'll see what is driving it."

At Thyme Tanneries ABC had also been tried, particularly in order to analyse marketing and distribution costs by customer. However, this analysis had revealed that the costs involved when expressed per square foot of product fell into a fairly narrow range so the exercise did not reveal information that would lead to policy changes.

At Tulip Tyres, ABC had been tried but abandoned because of its complexity. "I think we probably tried to go too far with it." However, the ideas inherent in activity-based analysis are still employed: "We also have the ability to analyse the fixed cost element of those costs if we need to: by market, by product, by whatever . . ."

And, at Apple Aeros, an activity-based exercise had been undertaken in the early 1990s but this seemed to be more concerned with process analysis than with costing.

Companies having an interest in activity-based costing (4 companies)

Perhaps the company most interested in ABC at the time of the interviews was Primrose Plastics, a subsidiary of a Dutch parent originally set up (by its parent) in the 1960s. This company adopts a contribution margin approach to management information and its parent had tried to eliminate the "overhead in stock" adjustment line. Now, however, with international accounting standards, other group companies are making the adjustment. At this company there is current interest in analysing indirect production, storage, distribution and commercial costs using activity-based methods. It seems that this company provides an example of interest in both contribution methods (the group preference) *and* ABC. The latter is not driven by a desire to "correct" existing absorption costs but by interest in analysing the profitability of business segments. In this analysis, non-production costs related to distribution and storage are to be investigated.

Our interviewee at Forget-me-not Foam was also clear about the possible advantages of an ABC analysis. Here again, a contribution style financial reporting layout had been adopted, this time driven by our interviewee, himself. He was obviously in favour of contribution accounting and did not like the absorption of overhead in stock for internal (or external) reporting. However, he set out the possible advantages of an activity-based analysis in exemplary style. "We have quite a big variety of products and processes and customers, they make certain demands on us and there is a big difference between the automotive accounts and the furniture accounts." Again the interest is not so much in "correcting" absorption costs as in investigating the profitability of certain segments of the business.

At Honesty Hydraulics our interviewee was familiar with ABC from his previous experiences. Even though Honesty Hydraulics is a comparatively small operation (turnover approximately £15 million per annum) and the scope for ABC to yield interesting insights was limited ". . . some people are quite keen".

At Carnation Cans the French parent company was attempting to introduce ABC throughout the group but our interviewee was, as yet, unconvinced of the value of this. "We're all a bit sceptical about the amount of time we're spending on inputting data and the lack of kind of the results we're getting out and the major assumptions that are being made to put that data in."

Companies that had consciously rejected activity-based costing (8 companies)

At Holly Health Furniture a traditional, full absorption costing system is employed together with gross profit-based financial reporting. The company is profitable and the existing system well understood. Our interviewee had considered ABC but: "We've never got excited about it really. It seems an awful lot of work [with] money for expensive people like Andersons and Price Waterhouse and computer models . . . focusing on your own navel."

At Shasta Ships our interviewee had used ABC "in a previous life" but it was not considered appropriate in this contracting business. Nevertheless, there was clearly some "activity-based thinking" in our interviewee's comments concerning the pricing of large contracts which were known to make proportionately less demand on the organisation's administrative resources.

At Sunflower Seals there was a similar reaction as our interviewee felt that ". . . I didn't think it was applicable here because of the nature of the products."

At Esther Enzymes, another company that undertakes major contracts, our interviewee also thought that ABC would be inappropriate. "I think the advantage of project accounting gives a level of complexity which means that ABC on top would be just too complex for what we need."

At Pine Packaging the principles of ABC are understood and the ideas are used in other parts of the group. However, the emphasis is on controlling wastage and "make ready" times, while areas such as selling and administration costs, where activity-based analysis might be useful, are a relatively unimportant element of cost.

At Cherry Components our interviewee had not used ABC: "Personally I'm not a believer, activity-based management I'm a great believer in but activity-based costing, [in] our environment I don't think it's particularly appropriate." Our interviewee added that he had not been impressed by demonstrations of ABC software.

At Robin Rectifiers it was not felt that ABC would be helpful. The company already sold through a very limited number of major customers and, in general, non-manufacturing overhead is small so there would not be great benefit from an ABC analysis. It is worth noting that, in this high-tech company, the resources and computer systems needed to implement ABC would not be an issue. The company employs very sophisticated analysis of sales which can be "sliced and diced" to provide a real-time analysis by product, customer, territory, etc.

At Daffodil Dairy the decision not to employ ABC was clearly personal as our respondent commented: "I didn't get on with ABC". (He had passed the book to his daughter who might get on with it better than he did!)

Comment

This anecdotal evidence suggests lukewarm support for activity-based techniques in the survey companies and is probably consistent with questionnaire-based surveys that have shown 10–20% of manufacturing companies interested in the technique. Often the reason given for lack of interest was the perceived lack of relevance of the technique in a particular context. There were also examples of personal antipathy to the technique (Daffodil Dairy), perceived complexity (Tulip Tyres, Esther Enzymes) and cost (Holly Health Furniture).

In general, reactions in the survey companies are consistent with other studies of the take-up of ABC and of issues in change management more generally. With some over-simplification successful change seems to require a good, technically feasible project with promising benefits in relation to cost; a champion; cultural acceptance by the project's users and top management support.

One can see, in these companies, that the possible introduction of ABC often falls at the first hurdle because it is expected not to be particularly relevant or too costly. In companies that have tried it, the system might be seen as too complex or the information generated not particularly useful.

There are also examples of lack of interest for want of a project champion with a number of interviewees appearing decidedly unconvinced. Perhaps the classic example is at Daffodil Dairy where it seems unlikely that ABC will be introduced by our interviewee! And, at Primrose Plastics, we were told that the introduction of ABC had been considered only recently because the previous Financial Director was of the "old school" and showed little interest in the technique.

Carnation Cans also seems not to have a champion for the ABC project. At this company, there is top management support for the project and (possibly) sufficient resources, but local management is unimpressed by the effort involved, assumptions made, or likely outcome of the project.

Activity-based costing is not really seen as *necessary* in most of the companies. Broadly they do not see the technique as important to inform decisions. They are either content with the fully absorbed costs already in use (for example at Willow Windows for transfer pricing and Apricot Aeros for price justification) or only use "full" costs for stock valuation and see other techniques as more important for informing decisions. There is little support, in this survey, for the "relevance lost" perspective that deemed full absorption costs to be misleading managers. At these companies, either full costs are used with some care and managers are aware of their drawbacks, or their use is limited and, typically, marginal cost methods are employed to inform decisions.

7.6 Influences on choice of reporting system

A number of influences on the design of reporting systems could be identified.

Production technology

Perhaps most obviously the impact of production technology and the type of business can be seen in contractors and in wholesalers/intermediaries. Contractors might opt for contribution or gross profit style financial formats but, either way, in the 4 "contracting companies" (Acacia Aerospace, Shasta Ships, Sunflower Seals, Esther Enzymes) there is heavy emphasis on contract profitability. And this is after allocating "full costs" to contracts.

The wholesalers/intermediaries (Cornflower Coated Steels, Tigerflower Tinplate, Campion Catalysts, Oak Oils) employ similar formats in their P&L reporting. In these companies, with limited manufacturing operations, "contribution" and "gross profit" are effectively reported by the same line in the P&L. Contribution by product group is important and further analysis may be undertaken if heavy technical or marketing costs can be attributed to product groups.

Information technology

Information technology can be an influence but not always a beneficial one. Larkspur Lighting, following rapid growth, introduced a new system but: ". . . we thought we got the right one and then it all went wrong." This company is now using its old systems ". . . until we get the courage up again . . .". And, at Tiger-lily Typing, ". . . we still haven't really got to grips with it [the system] . . . there's some weird postings happen there in the manufacturing side which we don't fully understand." Sometimes an "old" MRP system might not be changed because, as at Holly Health Furniture, it is deemed adequate.

Parental influence

Parental influence was an important factor in a number of companies. Primrose Plastics has seen little change to its group mandated system in the past ten years[27]. Acacia Aerospace introduced an integrated system, incorporating MRP, in 1998, harmonising its systems with those of group. Shamrock Shelving and Daisy Drinks expect to see their MRP systems upgraded in line with group policy within 18 months. In the latter case a relatively recent takeover by a US multinational drives policy. Group influence could be observed in the SAP and ABC initiatives at Carnation Cans. Group lays down the P&L format and the standard MRP system at Cherry Components. And, at Heather Health Equipment, the switch to simple systems (over-simple in the view of our interviewee) has been group-driven and "It's the tightest company I've worked in. In subtle ways you don't realise you're being controlled but you are."

---

[27]However, the company has an "open software" policy, allowing functional choice of systems but interfacing these. For example, the MRP system feeds directly into the financial reporting package, CODA.

Depth of analysis

Desire for greater analytical sophistication could be observed in some companies. This was most obvious at Pine Packaging where a contribution style format is adopted but "full job costs" are planned to inform decision-making. The "Gallic" influenced companies Carnation Cans and Bluebell Building Products also seem to be planning more sophisticated systems. At Carnation Cans, having introduced a SAP system, both ABC and standard costing initiatives are under consideration.

Other companies (most obviously Thyme Tanneries, Tulip Tyres and Forget-me-not Foam) prefer simplification. At Thyme Tanneries, dissatisfaction with traditional standard costing was a driver of change (now used as an "indicator of trends" and not for much else) while Tulip Tyres and Forget-me-not Foam had consciously introduced contribution margin systems. At Tulip Tyres: ". . . we wanted our P&L to reflect more closely the way we made our decisions" and, at Forget-me-not Foam: "The thing is it's fairly simple you know it's not trying to over complicate things. I mean at the end of the day you know business is all about communication and you have to get that message across."

Form of analysis

Desire for certain types of cost analysis, typically into fixed and variable components or in line with "cost objects" such as product groups, market segments, etc. was an important driver in many companies. "Contribution companies" are often influenced by a desire for meaningful product unit or segmental information. This driver can also be seen in the "absorption costing companies" where analysis below the gross profit line allows performance of sales channels, "platforms", etc. to be disclosed.

Size and autonomy

In small companies individual preferences and particular attitudes can have an important impact. Most obviously, at Elm

Engineering and Larkspur Lighting the managing director and the managing director/owner respectively have conservative attitudes that influence their desire to "write it all off" and not to "fake the value of stock".

In some companies there were individuals who had sufficient autonomy to make their own reporting choices. The (contribution-oriented) decisions at Thyme Tanneries, Tulip Tyres, Forget-me-not Foam and Marigold Medical could be traced to personal preference, typically of the financial controller.

Very subjectively, we have the impression that large companies, with a heavy manufacturing (as opposed to service) orientation that are part of major multinational groups tend to employ stand-ard absorption costing systems. The justification of prices to major customers could be important in these companies as could the use of "full costs" as a basis for transfer pricing.

"Best practice"

There was a hint in some companies, that the financial controller had a view of "best practice". At Shamrock Shelving we have the impression that the system "ought" to incorporate all variances (including variable overhead) and overhead recovery rates "should" be matched to the collection of actual costs. The idea of "best practice" did not necessarily lead to absorption costing. At Forget-me-not Foam, our interviewee was ". . . CIMA trained and basically I believe that is the correct way, I believe direct costs are direct costs and the direct costs [in] manufacturing are materials, labour and transport."

External financial reporting standards

A major conclusion is that many survey companies have a prefer-ence for contribution style reporting. However, despite the many examples of contribution formats the influence of financial reporting requirements can be discerned in the methods used, in many companies, to adjust stock values and net profit in *internal* financial reporting.

While particular systems might be influenced by a variety of factors[28], the requirements of external financial reporting sit like an eminence grise above, behind and within system choices and can overlay or over-ride other "systems drivers". Our initial reaction, on seeing the extensive use of contribution concepts in the survey companies was to see this as refuting the "relevance lost" thesis of management accounting. If most "contribution companies" do not use full absorption costs (much), then the relevance lost view of misleading, financial accounting oriented, full product costs is refuted in these companies. The fact that few companies are interested in the "improved absorption costs" of first wave ABC also tends to refute the view that traditional absorption costs are a problem. However, *many* of the "contribution companies" introduce P&L adjustments so that net profit is reported on an absorption cost basis. In *this* respect, external financial reporting requirements intrude into internal reporting.

While marginal costing companies might be influenced by external financial regulations, but *not* because of the use of inappropriate full product costs, full absorption costing companies may have more of a case to answer. In these companies, full absorption costs might be inappropriately used and, possibly, segmental analyses might be tainted by the inclusion of manufacturing fixed costs in establishing "gross profit" by segment.

We return to these issues in the final chapter but, first, we report the methods of budgeting, forecasting and evaluation used in the survey companies. We shall see that external financial regulation can impact on internal practices in other ways.

---

[28]Only some of which are captured by the usual contingency theory variables: perceived environmental uncertainty, size, technology, centralised/decentralised, strategy, etc. Even if some correlation is found between some of these variables we are not sure what advice can be given to practising managers and accountants given the rather abstract nature of the constructs involved.

Budgets, Forecasts and Performance Evaluation

8.1 Introduction

Budgeting in some form was prevalent in all but one of the companies studied, the exception being Daffodil Dairy, a company that adopts simple management reporting based on closure of its financial ledgers. Budgeting appears to be a fairly routine and predictable activity in the survey companies and is quickly dealt with in Section 8.2. Approaches to forecasting are, by contrast, more varied with different forecast periods and frequency of forecast updates. Section 8.3, describing these methods is therefore longer and more complex than Section 8.2. We then turn, in Section 8.4, to the *use* of budgets and forecasts, in particular, as comparators to the actual results reported in the financial statements. Finally, in Section 8.5, we deal with the evaluation of managers in the survey companies. Most employ bonus schemes of some sort and, usually, these are financially based or have an important financial component.

There are issues of terminology, with some companies referring to a "plan" and using the terms "forecast" and "budget" interchangeably. However, for clarity, in this chapter we define the budget as an initial plan of performance that is agreed before the financial year.

8.2 Budgeting

Daffodil Dairy is the only company not to set a budget and appears to have no scientific way of checking the progress of the organisation: "They work on a ... hope that everything is going to come out all right. But month my month they don't know." Although management in this company is sometimes taken by surprise when actual profit is reported, there is little management interest in budgeting or forecasting. Perhaps, at Daffodil Dairy, a cash rich environment coupled with the knowledge and experience of the owning family has meant that formal budgeting is perceived as an expensive luxury. However, our interviewee was trying: "... to interest our folks in forecasts" and new accounting software might facilitate budgeting and forecasting in future. A month-by-month comparison with the previous year to understand any possible trends was also under consideration. Thus, even in the one survey company that did not ostensibly use budgets, budget forecast and prior year analyses were under consideration.

The remaining 40 companies all produce a budget, usually as part of a standardised annual procedure. Only three companies diverge significantly from the typical annual routine, Cherry Components, Esther Enzymes and Larkspur Lighting. The first two update their budgets more frequently than once per year while Larkspur Lighting operates two budgets.

Cherry Components has a formal budgeting process that operates on a six-month cycle. This company produces a new (twelve-month) budget every six months and submits this to the Head Office for approval. On approval the first six months in the budget is fixed and becomes the basis for comparison with actual results. However, the second six months is provisional, to be replaced in the next six monthly cycle of budgeting. Similarly, Esther Enzymes adopts a biannual process. In this company a budget is set for twelve months together with a projection for the following two years, and this is revised after six months. ". . . we do formally call it a 'budget 2', so we re-set it, we don't just slavishly follow the original budget."

Larkspur Lighting is exceptional in formally recognising the existence of two budgets, a sales budget based upon the sales quantity set by the Sales Director and an operational budget. "We're running two separate budgets because we've got what the sales director said he could get so that's the target he's given his sales people and then we've got the accounts budget that is set about 10% lower." The sales budget operates as a target for the sales force while the operational budget is used in the P&L when making comparisons between actual and budget results.

Apart from Cherry Components and Esther Enzymes we could see little evidence of companies updating their budgets during the financial year. Most of the survey companies set a budget for the financial year and do not amend it.

Concluding thoughts

With only one company *not* producing a budget, budgeting is widely accepted in the companies in this survey. Even at the one exceptional, family owned company there is interest in more sophistication based on budgets and forecasts.

Whilst companies are producing budgets, there is little evidence of advanced techniques that go "beyond budgeting". Only three companies appear to diverge from standard, annual, budgeting practices, one company producing both sales and operational budgets and the others producing a hybrid forecast and budget, effectively a biannual 12-month rolling forecast/budget.

8.3 Forecasting

Some of the early, pilot, companies were not asked whether they undertook routine forecasting and there were some interviewees who were unable to answer this question. However, of the 34 companies that were able to respond, 31 routinely undertook forecasting of some sort (see Table 8.1).

Analysis of the frequency with which forecasts are revised in the 31 companies for which information is available is set out in Table 8.2.

The following analysis draws together information from these two tables, working through the classifications set out in Table 8.1 and integrating analysis of forecasting frequency as appropriate.

Table 8.1: Analysis of forecasting undertaken

Forecasting	Number of companies
Companies not asked or unable to discuss forecasting[29]	7
No forecast	3
Forecast to year-end	17
Rolling forecast	9
Combined rolling and year end forecasts	3
Forecast to end of following year	1
Current month forecast only	1
Total	41

---

[29]Flying Foods, Aster Autovending, Marigold Medical, Willow Windows, Elm Engineering, Iris Instruments and Apple Aeros.

Table 8.2: Analysis of forecasting frequency (31 companies)	
Frequency of forecasting	*Number of companies*
Biannual	3
Quarterly or three times per year	15
Monthly	8
Weekly *and* quarterly	1
Monthly *and* quarterly	3
Quarterly *and* ad hoc	1

Companies that do not prepare forecasts (3 companies)

The 3 companies that do not prepare forecasts are Daffodil Dairy, Larkspur Lighting and Tiger-Flower Tinplate. Daffodil Dairy has simple systems, but nevertheless is interested in developing budgeting and forecasting. Tiger-Flower Tinplate is undergoing a number of changes stemming from the introduction of a new computerised accounting system. As a result, forecasting will soon be introduced: "To be honest that's our next step. For example I have to prepare a forecast this month for next month. It's just beginning to kick in now. . . ." Larkspur Lighting does not produce formal forecasts, partly because they might become available to the company's bank. However, the financial controller makes calculations for the directors to check the effect of certain changes such as price adjustments. Thus, even the 3 companies that do not routinely prepare forecasts have an interest in doing so.

Companies that produce forecasts to the end of the financial year (17 companies)

Of the 31 companies that routinely produce forecasts, the majority (17) concentrate their forecasting on the current financial year. These forecasts are often referred to as "3 + 9" (3 months actual plus 9 months forecast), "6 + 6" (6 months actual plus 6 months forecast), "9 + 3" (9 months actual plus 3 months forecast) and so on. The degree of detail ranges from a full complement of performance measures to comparatively simple cash forecasting. Most companies reforecast every 3 or 4 months.

Some companies, such as Campion Catalysts and Fir Films, do not have a standard frequency for updating their forecast but we could identify 10 companies that have formal quarterly forecasting routines: Holly Health Furniture, Tulip Tyres, Sunflower Seals, Shamrock Shelving, Fuschia Fabrics, Daisy Drinks, Apricot Aeros, Honesty Hydraulics, Peony Prosthetics and Carnation Cans. Poppy Plasterboard also forecasts three times per year but not on a quarterly timetable.

The procedures can be highly structured as at Holly Health Furniture where forecasts are referred to as "prognoses" and it is the third "prognosis" that gets most attention "Yes and they focus on P3 [prognosis 3] a lot. I mean there's conference calls go on ... you know 'why aren't you going to be better?' That's always the question." Tulip Tyres provides another example of sophisticated procedures with detailed quarterly forecasts, including analysis of prices, costs, product groups and markets. A supplementary forecast at a much lower level of detail is also prepared for the following financial year. In addition to these forecasts, there is a high level review every month, taking into consideration any major changes (but not amending the forecasts). And Poppy Plasterboard's parent-driven schedule requires forecasts at the end of months 5 and 9, with a third forecast at the beginning of month 12 "Basically that has to be the same, or that is effectively the same, as the year-end result ... We do this final forecast about the second week of month 12, basically we stop trading a week thereafter, so they know exactly what's going to hit them ... It's very planned." This practice is convenient in a large multi-national but only practicable if trading can be suspended for a short space of time.

There is one company, Acacia Aerokit, that usually forecasts only once during the financial year, after 6 months, although: "Obviously if there are any downturns then people become more interested so you may be having to do it more often." Relatively infrequent forecasting does not mean it is unimportant in this company with monthly comparisons between actual and forecast results.

As we noted, Tulip Tyres undertakes some monthly forecasting in addition to its formal quarterly forecasts and there was evidence of this is in Peony Prosthetics and Carnation Cans as well. At Peony Prosthetics a detailed cash flow forecast is produced every month, largely driven by the high importance of cash: "The company has got into a position whereby cash is somewhat more important than profit at the moment." At Carnation Cans quarterly full year forecasts are required by the French parent but monthly forecasts for the forthcoming month are also produced for internal management.

Three companies routinely update their full year forecasts every month: Oak Oils, Bluebell Building Products and Forget-me-not Foam. Interviewees in these companies gave the impression that forecasting is driven by local management rather than by group requirements.

Month by month re-forecasting at Oak Oils allows continuous comparisons of full-year forecasts "Not saying that we ignore all the plan [budget] . . . but it's looking at the variances between one forecast and the next is the key." (As the budget becomes out of date, comparisons between the monthly full-year forecasts become increasingly important.)

At Bluebell Building Products (a subsidiary of a French multinational) monthly forecasting ensures some realism in financial projections, "The budgets that are set tend to be set, well they're so optimistic it's almost slightly funny . . . You look at the numbers they're coming up with and you know that they will never ever achieve them they're so unrealistic." At this company cash flow forecasting is also important: ". . . the main reason we do the forecast is to estimate our cash flow."

Realism is also a driving force at Forget-me-not Foam, another subsidiary of a large multi-national. Here, the budget is considered "an achievable target but it's a challenging target" whereas the forecast is more realistic ". . . the forecast is really a bit more of a realistic, well okay we're now running at a rate of whatever, so the forecast and the actual should be as close as possible".

Perhaps the need for realism and cash flow pressures are driving forces in companies that undertake frequent forecast revisions.

Companies preparing rolling forecasts (9 companies)

There are nine companies that produce rolling forecasts, typically for a year ahead and usually re-forecasted on a quarterly basis. Six companies produce rolling twelve month forecasts: Cornflower Coated Steel, Robin Rectifiers, Petunia Plastics, Shasta Ships, Esther Enzymes and Thyme Tanneries. The first four of these companies re-forecast every quarter while Esther Enzymes usually re-forecasts only once per year, and, at the other extreme, Thyme Tanneries calculates a 12 month rolling forecast "at least once a month".

Although they all produce rolling twelve-month forecasts there is considerable diversity of practice within these companies.

For example, it would be easy to overestimate the importance of forecasting at Petunia Plastics and Thyme Tanneries. At Petunia Plastics: "I don't think we used to reforecast before we were taken over." And, for internal comparative analyses, Petunia Plastics continues to use the original budget. At Thyme Tanneries, although the forecast is for a full year "the remainder of the [financial] year is really the bit that anyone takes any notice of."

On the other hand, forecasting could be underestimated at Robin Rectifiers, Shasta Ships and Esther Enzymes. In contrast to Petunia Plastics, at Robin Rectifiers, forecasts are used in preference to the original budget in making comparisons with actual results. At Shasta Ships, forecasting is *very* important. Not only is there a quarterly twelve month rolling forecast, there is also a forecast for the next three months produced *every week* and individual project performance is reviewed twice each week. Finally, at Esther Enzymes, although a full forecast is produced only once a year, this is soundly based: "Because our contracts are long term in nature, well most of them, we can predict invoicing and cash receipt points so we have quite a good forward view of potential cash receipts."

The remaining 3 companies, Everlasting Extinguishers, Heather Health Equipment and Tiger-lily Typing, produce rolling forecasts for shorter time periods, six, six and three months respectively. At Everlasting Extinguishers a high-level six month rolling forecast is produced every month from the Managing Director's estimates: "We have what we term as the MD's forecast, he forecasts what we're going to do in sales and profit for the next six months." Finance seem to be little involved, given that: ". . . if we did a forecast we would basically be taking each month [actual] and just adding budget." At Heather Health Equipment a forecast is produced every six months for the next six months but: "The main thing we're judged on is last year." At Tiger-lily Typing a three-month rolling forecast is revised monthly. *However*, in addition, there are forecasts to the next "milestone": half year and year end.

At Tiger-lily Typing our interviewee also spoke about the use of short-term forecasts as part of the 10 day monthly reporting cycle. These are referred to as "snap" forecasts, produced on the second working day of month-end procedures. Supposedly the SNAP forecast is an estimate but: ". . . the main board of Directors, when they meet we don't actually produce the [actual] results, so they tend to look at the snap and regard them as being actual . . . it's only an estimate but there's always hell to pay if you're a million miles away from your estimate."

Companies preparing both financial year and rolling forecasts (3 companies)

Three companies, Rose Resins, Primrose Plastics and Pine Packaging combine both rolling and full-year forecasts. Both Rose Resins and Primrose Plastics complete a rolling three month forecast every month and produce year-end forecasts as one-off, ad hoc exercises. Pine Packaging combines the two forecasts in a different way. They produce an overall forecast to the year-end and a rolling forecast just at plant level. The overall forecast is completed at the end of months 6 and 9 and the rolling forecast every 3 months for the next 12 months.

Companies forecasting to the end of the following year (1 company)

One company, Flax Fans, had probably gone further than the other survey companies, forecasting for up to two years ahead, to the end of the following financial year. The Managing Director of this company (a qualified accountant) undertook Masters studies at the University of the West of England and therefore the authors are aware of the changes that have been introduced in relation to presentation of forecasts at Flax Fans. The managing director wished to improve the presentation of accounts and, after consultation with the management team, eventually settled on graphical presentations that included the previous and current year results and forecasts for the remainder of the current year and the following year. Readers interested in these developments will find them set out in more depth in the section of the appendix devoted to Flax Fans, pages 53–55.

Companies producing a current month forecast (1 company)

Like Tiger-lily Typing, Cherry Components also creates forecasts for the current month. At this company the biannual budget obviates some of the need for forecasting, as the budget itself is similar to a biannual 12-month rolling forecast. Nevertheless: "Our MD likes to have a forecast at the end of each month. Just before the end and he compares the actual result with the forecast." Although Cherry Components does not have a formal quarterly forecasting process the creation of the mid-year budgeting process starts at the end of month 3, when half year and full year estimates are calculated.

Concluding thoughts

Virtually all the survey companies asked, confirmed that they produce forecasts and, of the 3 companies not currently producing forecasts, only Larkspur Lighting have no plans to do so.[30]

Although there is considerable variation in forecasting methods it is clear that great emphasis is placed on current financial year forecasting; 17 of 31 "forecasting companies" prepare forecasts only to the end of the current financial year. And, even in companies that generate rolling forecasts, it is clear that financial year forecasting can be important, if not paramount. At Tulip Tyres the extra 12 months beyond the current year are forecast in considerably less detail than the current year. At Thyme Tanneries the rest of the year: "is really the bit that anyone takes any notice of". And at Tiger-Lily Typing and Shasta Ships relatively short-run rolling forecasts are supplemented by full year forecasts. There is plenty of evidence that companies are concerned, in their financial forecasting and planning, with results for the current financial year. We see this as evidence of financial regulation impacting internal management control systems and, in this case, it is likely that the impact is so taken for granted that managers hardly even consider the impact that it might have.

---

[30]And even Larkspur Lighting produce rudimentary forecast calculations should prices be changed.

"Parental" influence was, again, plain in some companies. Where systems are well defined and institutionalised, a parent company's influence could sometimes be discerned, for example at Carnation Cans, Holly Health Furniture, Poppy Plasterboard and Petunia Plastics. Additionally there was some evidence of companies choosing to prepare "realistic" internal forecasts as an antidote to the optimistic budgets agreed or imposed by their parent companies.

We conclude that budgeting and forecasting is commonplace in UK manufacturing companies with virtually all companies in this survey preparing budgets and the majority supplementing these with regular forecasts.

8.4 Making sense of financial performance: Segmental and comparative analyses

Introduction

The 41 companies interviewed all provided a sample of their internal P&L. However, not all the formats allowed us to check which comparisons (actual results versus budget, forecast, etc.) were routinely undertaken. Some companies, such as Flying Foods, Tiger-lily Typing, Rose Resins and Campion Catalysts provided segmental P&Ls analysed by division, product group or business unit and, in this format, there was no comparison between actual results, budget, forecast, etc. The next two sub-sections deal, first, with those companies that provided us with a "segmental" P&L then, in the following section, we analyse P&Ls that concentrate on comparison between actual results and various comparators: budget, forecast, etc.

Three companies, Oak Oils, Thyme Tanneries and Apple Aeros, supplied P&Ls that provided neither an analysis by business segment nor an analysis that showed actual results in relation to comparators such as budget or forecast. These 3 companies are therefore excluded from the following analysis. On the other hand, two companies (Fuschia Fabrics and Cherry Components) supplied information that showed their interest in analysis *both* by business segment and by comparison to budget, forecast, etc. These two companies are therefore included in both the following sections.

Table 8.3: P&Ls analysed by segment (10 companies)	
Analysis	*Number of companies*
Business unit/Market segment	3
Business unit/Division	2
Division/Sales territory	1
Product group within divisions	1
Product group	2
Outlets	1

P&Ls designed to report segmental performance (10 companies)

It can be seen from Table 8.3 that 10 companies supplied P&Ls that highlight analysis by some aspect of the business. Six companies indicated that there were divisions within their organisation. In 3 of these companies the divisions are focused on market segments and in one company on sales territories. Three of the other four companies focus their reports on product groups while one company directs its analysis to distribution channels (outlets).

P&Ls designed to report "current month" and "year-to-date" comparisons (30 companies)

It can be seen from Table 8.4 that all 30 companies in this group report actual results for the period and most (28), but not all, report cumulative, year-to-date, actual results. The exceptions are Cherry Components and Pine Packaging.

Table 8.4: Comparison of actual results with budget, forecast, etc. in the P&L (30 companies)		
Item	*Number of companies reporting period data*	*Number of companies reporting cumulative data*
Actual result	30	28
Budget	20	19
Variance to budget	15	18
Forecast	7	2
Variance to forecast	5	3
Previous year	12	16
Variance to previous year	4	6

The majority (20) of these companies include the period budget in their P&L presentation and 17 of these 20 companies also include the year-to-date budget. Additionally there are companies that record the variance between actual and budget, so the budget is implicitly included in the presentation. Tiger-flower Tinplate, Heather Health Equipment and Honesty Hydraulics fall into this category, all 3 reporting variance versus budget for both period and year to date.

We conclude that the reporting of period and year-to-date results and comparison of these to budget is important in these 30 companies, 23 (77%) undertake this analysis for the period and 22 (73%) undertake the corresponding analysis for the year to date. Although there are 3 companies carrying out periodic but not year-to-date analysis, conversely, there are two companies, Carnation Cans and Apricot Aeros, that do not undertake periodic analysis, but do carry out year-to-date analysis. If we count companies that *either* report period budgets/variances *or* year-to-date budgets/variances then in this group of 30 companies there are 25 (83%) that employ actual/budget reporting in their P&Ls.

What of the five companies that do not compare actual with budget figures, either explicitly or implicitly? One company, Marigold Medical simply does not have a comparative analysis, either for period or year-to-date figures. This company does, though, present year-to-date actual figures together with the current month and the forecast for each remaining month in the year. Two companies, Tulip Tyres and Robin Rectifiers, prefer to make their comparisons against forecast rather than budget. And two companies, Holly Health Furniture and Larkspur Lighting, compare their results to those of the previous year rather than budget.

We conclude that, although a number of interviewees claimed that forecasts are more important than budgets (because the latter are "out of date") where documentary evidence is available, there is a tendency to make comparisons against budget, not forecast. This conclusion appears to be reinforced by the observation that only seven companies report period forecasts/variances and only three report year-to-date forecasts/variances. Matters are not quite so simple, however, if those companies that incorporate *full-year* forecasts into their reports are also taken into account; then there are twelve companies that report forecast information in some form in their P&L. Even so, there are 25 companies in this group that report budgets or comparisons to budget while only twelve report month, year-to-date or full-year forecasts.

If there is relatively limited reporting of forecasts and forecast variances there are rather more companies making comparisons with previous year data. Twelve companies report the period results from the previous year and 17 (more than 50% of the companies in this group) report cumulative data for the previous year. We noted that two companies concentrate on prior year rather than budget comparisons and our interviewee at Holly Health Furniture commented: "All we compare is this year to last year . . . they're always focusing on last year because that's the way the stock market seems to work."

Some companies include full (financial) year data in their routine P&L reporting with Shasta Ships, Holly Health Furniture and Elm Engineering reporting a "full set" of full-year budget and forecast together with last year for comparison. And Fuschia Fabrics effectively reports this data by including full-year forecast versus last year variance. Carnation Cans (full-year budget), Larkspur Lighting (full-year forecast plus last year) and Robin Rectifiers (full-year forecast) report subsets of this data. Thus 7 of the survey companies systematically provide some data concerning the full year with six of these ensuring that the latest full-year forecast is presented routinely as part of the periodic accounts.

Finally, we note that there is a group of 7 companies: Everlasting Extinguishers, Cornflower Coated Steel, Bluebell Building Products, Larkspur Lighting, Heather Health Equipment, Petunia Plastics and Forget-me-not Foam that routinely report a different sort of analysis, elements of cost as a percentage of sales. In two of these companies it was clear that this analysis provided key information to managers. Our interviewee at Everlasting Extinguishers confirmed the importance of the analysis which is "definitely used". And, at Cornflower Coated Steel: "So that gross margin is a key indicator for us and also variable costs as well because those in our assessment are controllable."

Concluding thoughts

The analysis in this section was not easy because there seem to be so many different forecast periods, frequencies, combinations of forecasts and frequencies and emphases in the survey companies.

Some companies provided business unit or segmental analysis rather than a P&L format that compared actual results with budget, forecast, etc. We have noted before that the documentation observed is probably sensitive to the precise question asked and, in the companies visited during the "pricing" phase of the project, the researchers were shown segmental rather than comparative analyses. Given this methodological issue we would not claim that some companies "prefer" segmental rather comparative analysis or vice versa. Instead we have proceeded on the basis that the two sets of companies simply provide different sorts of insights into the reporting processes in manufacturing companies.

Whereas the segmental analyses are hardly surprising, concentrating on market segments, territories, channels, divisions and product groups, the comparative analyses are more interesting. Despite the considerable emphasis on forecasting in the survey companies, the P&L formats we received overwhelmingly emphasised comparisons to the original "fixed" budget rather than to forecast.[31] Only two companies preferred to compare actual results to forecast rather than budget.

Our overall impression is that the survey companies are influenced by the "technology" of budgeting with its predominantly annual management rhythm and external financial pressures. The latter appear in the emphasis, in many companies, on financial year forecasting and on comparisons with previous year results. More survey companies routinely report previous year results than current year forecasts. It is not difficult to find anecdotal evidence to support the view that companies respond to external pressures in their internal management. Our interviewee at Holly Health Furniture felt that comparison of current with previous year was important "... because that's the way the stock market seems to work." At Aprocot Aeros our interviewee simply felt that a "... quoted company lives or dies by [its] annual results and they [group headquarters] don't give a xxxx about next year, [only results] for the city this year". At Bluebell Building Products: "It's strange when we have any of the

---

[31]Only one interviewee, at Robin Rectifiers, mentioned "flexing" the fixed budget to take account of changes in volumes. The procedure at Robin Rectifier is rather sophisticated with line items given a flex factor that ranges from zero (truly fixed) to 1 (varies proportionately to sales).

reviews . . . they only look at prior year . . .". But, at Carnation Cans: "We believe that the only way ultimately to please our bosses is to deliver the results we've committed to in the budget."

It seems that, once a budget is set, it is expected to be delivered and forecasting is often a (financial year) focused technique that helps in the achievement of the over-riding objective, meeting the (short-term) expectations of senior management and the financial markets.

8.5   Performance measurement and remuneration

Introduction

Three of the early pilot companies, Marigold Medical, Flax Fans and Iris Instruments, were not asked whether they employed bonus schemes and this section is therefore based on responses from 38 companies. Remarkably (we think), 34 (89%) of these companies employ bonus incentive schemes of some sort. Of these 34 companies, 13 operate both executive and staff bonus schemes, 5 operate only an executive bonus scheme and 16 operate only a staff bonus scheme.

Executive bonus schemes (18 companies)

Analysis of the 18 executive bonus schemes revealed that the two most important measures are "profit versus budget or target" and "personal performance"; 10 companies use the former measure and 8 companies the latter (Table 8.5).

There was one company where our interviewee could not provide details of the executive bonus scheme. In the remaining 17 companies, 7 companies employ a single performance measure while 10 use a combination of measures.

In the 7 companies that employ a single indicator, 3 base executive bonuses on personal performance. The other 4 companies employ profit share, profit versus budget/target, sales and return on capital employed respectively as the single measure of performance.

In the 10 companies that employ a combination of measures, 9 use profit versus budget or target. Five of these combine this measure with personal performance. Two of these 5 companies add a third

Table 8.5: Analysis of performance indicators in executive bonus schemes (18 companies)	
Performance measure	Number of companies
Profit versus budget/target	10
Personal performance	8
Return on capital employed	3
Cash flow	3
Cost reduction	3
Profit growth	2
Profit share	1
Sales	1
Working capital	1
Health and safety	1

measure, cash flow and working capital, respectively. Four companies combine profit versus budget or target with a variety of measures. Two companies base their scheme on profit versus budget/target, cash flow and cost control; one company uses profit versus budget/target and profit growth; and one company uses profit versus budget/target, return on capital employed and cost control.

Finally, there is one company that bases its executive bonus scheme on two performance measures that do not include profit targets. Rose Resins uses return on capital employed and health and safety measures in its scheme.

Comments

Of 38 companies asked, approximately half (18) employ executive incentive schemes. The most popular performance measures are "profit versus budget or target" and "personal performance", 13 of the 18 companies employ one or both of these measures. A number of different performance measures were mentioned although four of these (profit share, sales target, working capital and health & safety) are used by only a single company. There was some support for return on capital employed, cash generation and cost control with 3 companies each using these measures. Interestingly, residual income and economic value added were not mentioned by any of the respondents describing their executive bonus schemes.

Perhaps the most striking feature of these schemes is their reliance on financial measures of performance. Profit share, profit target and profit growth appear as measures in 11 companies and these are regularly combined with more financial measures: cash flow, return on capital employed, cost control and working capital. There are just 3 companies, Larkspur Lighting, Apricot Aeros and Apple Aeros, that use solely personal performance and these schemes therefore do not have a financial component.

Overall we conclude that executive bonus schemes are quite prevalent in the survey companies but they are relatively simple. Typically they employ profit-based performance measures but the measures are unsophisticated with only 3 companies using return on capital employed and none using residual income or economic value added. There is very little use of non-financial performance measures with only one company using an explicit non-financial measure, a health and safety index, although 8 companies include "personal performance" in their schemes. Broadly, we think that the executive bonus schemes used are consistent with the emphasis on budgets and short-term performance highlighted in the previous section.

"Staff" bonus schemes (29 companies)

Analysis of the 29 companies that operate staff bonus schemes reveals that the most popular performance measure is "profit versus budget or target" with 15 companies adopting this measure (Table 8.6). A further 8 companies have profit-sharing schemes and one company includes profit growth in its scheme so, of 29 staff bonus schemes, 24 explicitly include profit as a performance measure.

There are 15 companies that use a single performance measure, 10 of these use profit versus budget or target, 4 employ profit-sharing schemes and one company (Daffodil Dairy) uses efficiency of production as its single performance measure.

There are 10 companies that employ combinations of measures that include either sales targets or efficiency of production. One might infer that these schemes tend to be targeted either at sales or production staff although two of these companies include both sales and efficiency of production in their package of measures. These

Table 8.6: Analysis of performance indicators in staff bonus schemes (29 companies)

Performance measure	Number of companies
Profit versus budget/target	15
Profit share	8
Efficiency of production	7
Sales	6
Personal performance	5
Cost control	4
On-time delivery	3
Wastage	2
Return on capital employed	2
Profit growth	1
Customer feedback	1
Innovation	1
Quality	1

schemes typically combine either sales or efficiency measures with personal performance, cost control, return on capital employed, etc.

The remaining 4 companies employ various combinations of profit versus budget/target, profit share, on-time delivery, cost control, customer feedback, quality and personal performance.

Although there are 15 companies that employ simple schemes based on a single performance measure there are also 14 companies that employ more sophisticated schemes. Five companies use two measures, 5 companies use three measures and 4 companies use four measures.

Comments

Of the 38 companies, 29 have staff bonus schemes. Most of these employ either "profit versus target or budget" or profit sharing as their primary method of determining bonus payments; 15 use the former measure and 8 the latter (with no overlap between these companies). For the remaining 6 companies, sales and efficiency of production are important measures with 5 of these companies using one or both of these measures. Fir Films is exceptional in not using profit, sales or efficiency measures. Nevertheless, Fir Films has one of the most complex schemes, based on four measures: personal performance, on-time delivery, cost control and quality.

Like the executive bonus schemes, the staff schemes place heavy emphasis on financial measures with 24 of 29 schemes including explicit, profit-based measures. Again like the executive schemes the profit measures are generally simple with only two companies using return on capital employed and none using residual income or economic value added. Again like the executive schemes, the staff bonus schemes might include other financial indicators although, additionally, in these schemes there is more use of non-financial indicators: wastage, on-time delivery, customer feedback, innovation and quality. Having said this these five indicators are used only in 6 companies so the emphasis of most schemes is still on financial performance. The staff schemes are probably a little more complex than executive schemes. Although 15 companies employ only a single performance measure, 14 companies employ multiple measures and 4 companies combine as many as four measures in calculating staff bonuses.

8.6 Conclusion

This chapter has provided a brief descriptive analysis of the budgeting, forecasting, reporting and evaluation methods employed in the survey companies. A fairly clear picture has emerged with virtually all the companies preparing budgets and most of those asked also preparing forecasts. Forecasting is institutionalised in a number of companies and is usually undertaken three times per year according to a predetermined schedule. However, despite the emphasis on forecasting it seems that, in most of the survey companies, comparisons are routinely made between actual results and a "fixed" budget. Only one interviewee drew our attention to "budget flexing" procedures, although, in that company, they seem quite sophisticated.

Somewhat unexpectedly most of the survey companies asked have implemented bonus incentive schemes. These are primarily financially oriented using relatively simple financial measures. Our survey did not pursue the extent to which companies employed "modern" techniques such as the balanced scorecard or economic value added. However, we can say that the measures employed in the ubiquitous incentive schemes described are largely financially oriented and relatively simple. None of the survey companies employ residual income or economic value added and only a few companies use return on capital employed as a performance measure.

We conclude that, typically, these companies have internal control systems based on traditional budgeting supported by financial year oriented forecasting routines and financially dominated incentive schemes. There is little evidence of techniques that go "beyond budgeting" in these companies and the emphasis on financial year reporting together with some of the comments made by interviewees persuades us that external pressures have real consequences in a number of these companies.

Conclusion

9.1 Introduction

This study has provided insights into the methods of accounting and internal financial reporting employed in some UK manufacturing companies at the beginning of the twenty-first century. The project was driven by the unexpected finding that, in 6 companies visited during an earlier project, companies appeared to be employing innovative reporting methods based on marginal cost, contribution style presentations. As the literature review in Chapter 2 demonstrates there is probably little that is really "new" in management accounting theory, and recommendations similar to the methods adopted in the pilot companies can be readily found in the literature (see Table 9.1).

Prior to the study the researchers believed that absorption costing, supported by the regulatory regime and the technologies of

Table 9.1: Segmental contribution statement (Wilson, 1999: 48) by kind permission of Thomson Learning

Product: Calculators	North territory (£)	South territory (£)	Total (£)
Net sales	xxx	xxx	xxx
Variable manufacturing costs	xx	xx	xx
Manufacturing contribution	xx	xx	xx
Marketing costs			
Variable			
Sales commissions	x	x	x
Selling expenses	x	x	x
Variable contribution	xx	xx	xx
Assignable			
Salespersons' salaries	x	x	x
Manager's salary	x	x	x
Product advertising	x	x	x
Product contribution	xx	xx	xx
Non-assignable			
Corporate advertising			x
Marketing contribution			xx
Fixed common costs			
Manufacturing			x
Administration			x
Net profit			xx

the 1970s and 1980s, continued to dominate direct costing. The evidence of Kaplan and his colleagues in the US and subsequent surveys in the UK appeared to confirm the prevalence of absorption costing. In this light, a key finding of this research is that, at the beginning of the twenty-first century, companies might be employing not absorption costing systems but marginal, contribution-based systems and this appeared to be "innovation".

Given that the practices observed had long been recommended, this led to some consideration of what "innovation" might mean in management accounting. First, it might mean that something completely new has been undertaken. Second and more usually, it might mean the introduction of something that is "new" to a particular company. And, third, it might relate to long-employed practices that are *not* new to the company but, because academic surveys have not revealed them previously, they are falsely thought to be innovative. We now believe that this last explanation is important in understanding the results of this study.

In the remainder of this chapter we review the research findings and their implications for views of manufacturing accounting practice at the beginning of the twenty-first century. We consider the implications for the relevance lost thesis of management accounting history and the conventional view of absorption costing "domination". Finally, we conclude with some comments on methodological issues in management accounting research.

9.2 Overview of research findings

Prevalence of marginal costing and contribution ideas

Our principal finding is that the main study confirms the impression gained in the pilot study that marginal costing and contribution ideas are used to a much greater extent in some UK manufacturing companies than expected. We conclude that 28 of the 41 survey companies employed contribution style reporting of some form, and if the definition of marginal cost/contribution reporting is relaxed, then the number employing these methods rises to 32.

As this finding is surprising, it was carefully checked by reference to the manner in which the "contribution companies" establish product costs. Most (20) of the contribution companies employ standard costs and their emphasis on *variable* cost variances confirms their emphasis on marginal costing and contribution analysis. Although 11 of these companies set overhead absorption rates and establish "full" standard costs these are usually used only in valuing stock. In the 8 "contribution companies" that do not set standards, their stock valuation methods are consistent with their contribution/marginal costing orientation. The researchers are satisfied that the 28 "contribution companies" have been correctly classified.[32]

Given that previous research has indicated a bias towards absorption costing in manufacturing companies we have to ask how this research could point towards such a different conclusion. We suggest three possible explanations. First, the ubiquitous references to gross profit and gross margin by companies that employ contribution concepts might have led to questionnaire survey-based research tending to underestimate the institutionalised use of marginal costs and contribution concepts in the UK manufacturing companies. In this survey, a number of companies use contribution concepts but do not name them as such. Second, several companies in this survey employ *both* marginal/contribution ideas *and* absorption costing based on overhead recovery rates. These systems might be "loosely coupled" in companies that employ contribution style presentations. If researchers "expect" to find absorption costing systems then the contribution style presentations of information might be overlooked. Third, prior literature does not rule out the use of marginal costing although this is easily overlooked. Drury *et al.* (1993) reported 52% of companies often/always using variable manufacturing cost for decision-making (p. 9). Additionally, a significant minority of 20% reported

---

[32]The authors were further reassured by the comments of a practitioner who reviewed the work prior to publication. In relation to contribution measures he or she made the following comment. "This was extremely interesting in that there is no right or wrong answer and often it depends on how businesses manage costs. In process manufacturing (my own industry) we are contemplating creating a sales contribution measure that excludes in house production overheads (labour, R&M, depreciation, etc.) but includes materials and contract packing fees (where they are integral to the product). Overhead recovery (including labour) could be left out of the contribution measure as sales do not actually control this cost and we want to see how much each unit of sales 'contributes' to paying for the divisional overheads."

that: "Only variable costs are traced to products and the total amount of fixed overhead incurred during the period is apportioned between inventory and the cost of goods sold" (p. 17).

Most companies set standards but many report actual costs

Further insights were obtained through questions about the use of standard costing in the survey companies. Most (70%) of the companies taking part in the study set standard costs and, for some of those that do not, the nature of their business means that it is unlikely that they would be interested in standard costing. Thus the widespread existence of standard costing in manufacturing businesses is confirmed and our results are consistent with those of Drury *et al.* (1993: 37).

However, analysis of variances calculated and their use in financial reporting causes us to have serious reservations concerning the extent of the *use* of standard costing systems. In several companies, standard costing systems provide a convenient means of valuing stock, but neither standards nor variances are particularly important in managing the business. This observation was further confirmed by analysis of the way financial results are presented. Of 30 companies that calculate standard costs, 17 either do not report standard cost of sales in their P&L account or report only a limited subset of (materials) variances. Of the 30 standard setting companies we therefore judge that over 50% limit their application.

Variance analysis important in some companies but overhead variances little used

Despite the limited use of variance analysis in P&L reporting most of the standard costing companies do calculate a variety of material and labour variances. A number of respondents confirmed the importance of particular variances. Material price variances are often calculated and used and, in some companies, such as Rose Resins and Daisy Drinks, analyses of material usage variances are important. Labour efficiency variances are also important in some companies and attempts to remove these variances as part of a lean manufacturing initiative at Apple Aeros ran into resistance from supervisors.

However, of the 30 companies that set standards, only 14 calculate overhead variances. Of these, 4 companies calculate only a single variable overhead variance and 6 calculate only a single "fixed" overhead variance. So the sophistication of overhead variances in these companies is very limited and just one company reports variable and fixed overhead variances analysed into rate, efficiency, spend and volume components. None of the survey companies analyses the overhead volume variance into its capacity and efficiency elements. This finding is starker even than that of Drury *et al.* (1993: 37) who found that: "Approximately 80% do not compute fixed overhead volume capacity and efficiency variances." This observation provoked those authors into wondering why these variances are still examined by professional bodies when they find so little favour with both practitioners and academics. The same can be said today.

Stock valuation procedures for external financial reporting compromise marginal costing principles in some companies

An advantage (perhaps *the* advantage) of following absorption costing principles in internal financial reporting is the congruence of internally reported stock values and profits with those reported externally. Thus the "absorption costing" companies do not usually need to make adjustments to the value of stock in preparing financial reports. Additionally, there are 10 survey companies that exclude manufacturing overhead from both their internally and externally reported stock values. This is acceptable for external reporting purposes in companies with immaterial levels of stock, intermediaries (wholesalers), contractors and companies like Pine Packaging that recognise revenue on production.

The remaining companies, following marginal costing principles, have to make adjustments in their accounts in order to ensure that external financial reports comply with accounting standards. Nine of these companies value stock at variable production cost in their internal management accounts and make annual or, in the case of Marigold Medical, infrequent, adjustments to stock value for external reporting purposes. Eleven companies follow marginal costing principles in their P&L presentation but include an adjustment line in the P&L that ensures that *internally* reported profit is consistent with external financial standards. Just one company, Tulip Tyres, reports net profit according to marginal costing principles but then makes the "overhead in stock" adjustment so that net profit is also reported on an absorption costing basis every month.

Approximately half of the companies in the survey make no adjustment to stock value for external reporting, either because they employ absorption costing systems for internal reporting or because they do not include manufacturing overhead in the value of stock in their external reports. The other companies make adjustments with 11 bringing their reported *internal* profit into line with external reporting requirements. These companies appear to compromise their marginal costing principles in order to ensure that internally reported profit is consistent with externally mandated standards.

Several companies attribute overhead to products and market segments

As we saw in Table 9.1 one of the advantages of a contribution format is the ease with which costs can be attributed to cost objects and a number of "contribution companies" use their reporting formats to do this. Although 5 companies show little interest in this analysis and 4 seem to be changing either their reporting formats or their organisation structures, 19 "contribution companies" undertake segmental analysis of some sort. Typical analysis is by product group, customer, region, sales channel or market segment.

Some companies actually structure their organisation around particular products or markets and, in these companies, financial reporting goes beyond just "analysis" because managers can be held responsible for results relating to particular products, markets, etc. We were impressed by "market facing" organisations that identify costs associated with each separate market segment. These companies report meaningful "contribution after sales and marketing costs" and the key to this analysis is not to apportion manufacturing overhead costs if this does not make sense. The aim is to generate sufficient contribution (from all the "market facing" business units) to cover manufacturing and other "fixed" overhead and make a healthy return on investment.

There were a few examples of overhead apportionment to business segments and some companies find this analysis useful. It is easy to see why a company such as Oak Oils, selling through several distribution channels, might wish to apportion/allocate marketing overhead to these channels. However, our interviewees were very familiar with the dangers of this sort of, often parent mandated, analysis. Treating the segmental "bottom line" net profit as meaningful could lead to ". . . a lot of manipulation because in Groups you get more manipulation than in parliament" (Cherry Components). Generally, overhead costs are allocated to business units, segments, markets etc only if this is obviously meaningful.

Practice at Tulip Tyres deserves special mention. This is the only company that reports monthly net profit on *both* marginal and absorption cost bases and, in addition, analyses contribution by four business units and, separately, by eight markets. Marketing is through sales companies and, recently, Tulip Tyres has introduced a system that provides full visibility of variable manufacturing costs to the sales companies. Sales companies receive commission on sales value and their performance is now evaluated against the contribution they generate.[33]

Companies that employ absorption costing systems also analyse their business by product group, business unit, etc. but their analysis begins not with manufacturing contribution but with manufacturing gross profit after deducting "full" manufacturing costs. In these companies some fixed costs are "hidden" above the gross margin line and this could distort product and market "profitability" analyses. However, none of our interviewees seemed concerned by this possibility.

No company was actually employing ABC at the time of the interviews although some companies had used it in the past and some of our interviewees had experience of ABC either in their current or in their former employments. In some companies there was interest in ABC, either because of parental pressure as at Carnation Cans or because our interviewee could see merit in the technique as at Heather Health Equipment.

---

[33] "Recent" developments at Tulip Tyres were recorded during a final conversation with our respondent during the summer of 2003.

Budgets almost universal and forecasting prevalent

Virtually all the survey companies asked, confirmed that they produce both budgets and forecasts and a significant number of "forecasting companies" concentrate their attention on the remainder of the financial year. There are routine procedures for budgeting and forecasting in most companies with greater diversity of practice in relation to forecasting. In some companies the routines had been laid down by the parent company. Our overall conclusion is that budgeting and forecasting practices are heavily institutionalised and often driven by senior management and external financial prerogatives with emphasis on routines designed to accommodate financial reporting cycles. Despite the emphasis on forecasting it seems that, in most of the survey companies, comparisons are routinely made between actual results and a "fixed" budget.

Despite the prevalence of forecasting comparisons are often made against budget

Some companies provided segmental P&Ls analysed by division, product group or business unit and, in this format, there was no comparison between actual results, budget, forecast, etc. Three of these companies focus on market segments, three on product groups, one on sales territories and one on distribution channels (outlets).

Thirty companies provided P&Ls that facilitate comparison between actual results and budget, forecast, etc. and almost all of these companies make comparisons between both period and year-to-date data. Most (25) of these companies make either period or year-to-date comparisons to budget. Fewer (only 12) include forecast data in their routine financial presentations although two of these explicitly preferred to make comparisons to forecast rather than budget. We conclude that, although a number of interviewees claimed that forecasts are more important than budgets (because the latter are "out of date") where documentary evidence is available, there is a tendency to make comparisons against budget, not forecast.

A significant number (17) of companies compare results to those of the previous year. At Holly Health Furniture our interviewee commented: "All we compare is this year to last year . . . they're always focusing on last year because that's the way the stock market seems to work."

Our overall impression is that the survey companies are influenced by the "technology" of budgeting with its predominantly annual management rhythm and external financial pressures. The latter appear in the emphasis, in many companies, on financial year forecasting and on comparisons with previous year results. More survey companies routinely report previous year results than current year forecasts.

Budgets, once set, need to be delivered and, despite budgets becoming outdated, comparisons are often made against this benchmark. Forecasting is often a (financial year) focused technique that helps in the achievement of the over-riding objective, meeting the (short-term) expectations of senior management and the financial markets.

Most companies employ incentive schemes

Remarkably (we think), 34 (89%) of these companies employ bonus incentive schemes of some sort. Of these 34 companies, 13 operate both executive and staff bonus schemes, 5 operate only an executive bonus scheme and 16 operate only a staff bonus scheme.

Of 18 companies employing executive bonus schemes, 13 include either "profit versus budget or target" or "personal performance". The use of financial measures is widespread but the profit measures are unsophisticated; only three companies use return on capital employed and none employ residual income or economic value added. Broadly we think that the executive bonus schemes used are consistent with the emphasis on budgets and short-term performance highlighted in the previous section.

Similarly, in the 29 companies that operate staff bonus schemes, the majority (24) explicitly include profit-related performance measures but, again, these are relatively unsophisticated comparisons to budget/target or profit sharing schemes, only two companies using return on capital employed and none using residual income or economic value added. Although 15 staff bonus schemes employ only a single performance measure, they are probably slightly more complex than executive bonus schemes with more non-financial measures and some companies using combinations of three or four measures.

9.3 The "Relevance Lost" view of management accounting history

In the literature review it was argued that the "relevance lost" analysis of management accounting history is not applicable in the UK for the following reasons.

First, in the US, Johnson and Kaplan claim "financial accounting domination" of management accounting from the early years of the twentieth century. In the UK there is little evidence of this until 1975 when SSAP9 effectively prohibited marginal costing for external reporting purposes. At the beginning of the twenty-first century more than 50% of survey companies are not inhibited (in this key respect) by external reporting standards.

Second, Johnson and Kaplan claim that, in the US, developments in management accounting seemed to stop about 1925. However, the passionate debates surrounding the development of direct or marginal costing indicate that cost accounting was hardly stagnating in the 1950s and 1960s (Dugdale and Jones, 2003).

Third, Johnson and Kaplan claim that existing (obsolete) costing systems were simply computerised in the 1960s and a great opportunity was missed to return to the "relevant" costing systems of earlier years. We question this for several reasons. First, it is not clear that "relevant" costing systems, in Johnson and Kaplan's terms, had been developed. We cannot see any difference, in principle, between the "scientific machine hour rates" developed by Church and the absorption rates that became prevalent in absorption costing systems during the twentieth century. Second, it is not clear that even the costing theory that had been developed was applied extensively in practice until the second half of the twentieth century.[34] In many companies even "obsolete" systems had not

---

[34]Boyns (1998) references Scapens (1991: 17) who felt that responsibility accounting was not taken up in UK companies until the 1950s and 1960s and Quail (1996) whose study "suggests that budgetary control methods made little impact in Britain before 1940" (p. 275). Tellingly, he also quotes a comprehensive survey of US companies by Black and Eversole (1946) that found that only 22% of US companies maintained cost records and only 2% used a standard costing system. Take-up of new systems might have been slow in both the UK and US.

yet been introduced! Third, the introduction of computer-based systems was no simple matter and the eventual development of sound MRP systems did not occur till the 1970s. These systems did not so much replicate existing systems as codify crystallising theory that now included, partly Inland Revenue driven, standard absorption costing.

Having said this, we accept that the (computer-based) absorption costing systems that Johnson and Kaplan criticised in the 1980s, suffered from the deficiencies ascribed to them. It was probably because practitioners could readily see the logic of the case made against existing absorption costing systems and for activity-based costing that the latter was so successfully marketed.

What are the implications of our view of cost accounting history and the results of this survey for the relevance lost thesis? We make two postulates. First, that absorption costing systems, as developed in the early years of the twentieth century, were relevant for some companies. As Vollmers (1996) has pointed out, from the 1920s to the 1950s, (US) texts were emphasising the importance of establishing overhead absorption rates for *each* homogeneous department. This recommendation is consistent with Church's system that appeared to find favour with Johnson and Kaplan. Second, we postulate that the direct or marginal costing systems developed in the 1950s and 1960s were also relevant for some companies. Then the relevance lost thesis can be restated as in Figure 9.1.

This analysis sets out more options than the Johnson and Kaplan diagnosis and prognosis. Johnson and Kaplan argued that cost accounting systems were irrelevant and something needed to be done. Their key recommendation was ABC. "Sophisticated" absorption costing was ignored, possibly because Harvard School researchers had not observed such systems during their (US-based) investigations in the 1980s. Direct or marginal costing was dismissed in a few lines:

> The financial reporting view of cost accounting was not challenged. The 1950s debate over "direct costing" shows the continuing dominance of the view. In that literature no one challenged the idea of attaching "integrated" costs to products. The debate merely focused on which costs to attach, full or direct. (Johnson and Kaplan, 1987: 139)

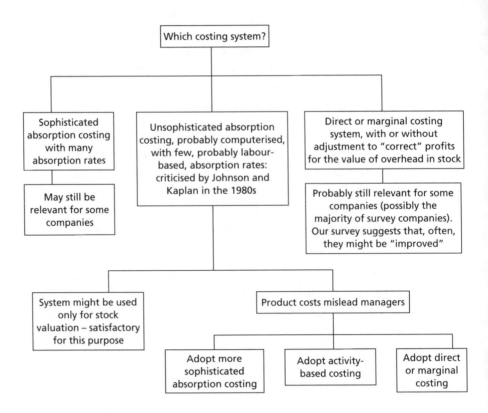

Figure 9.1 Which costing system?

At that time, Kaplan would have had little truck with marginal costing (see Jones and Dugdale, 2002). He believed that all costs are variable (except idle capacity and investment expenses) and should therefore be traced to product. However, sloughing off direct costing because it is based on the integration of accounts hardly does the subject justice. The key issue is not integration, but whether and how costs are to be attached to products.[35] The direct costers argued (and continue to argue) that it is pointless to apportion/allocate fixed overhead to products and this is the key to their case, not whether the method is or is not integrated with financial accounting.

---

[35]The integration of cost and financial accounts would presumably not pose a problem for Johnson and Kaplan if *activity-based* costs were integrated with the financial accounts.

With the benefit of hindsight we believe that, while the case made in "Relevance Lost" was pertinent for those companies that had adopted unsophisticated absorption costing systems, it over-simplified cost accounting history and the range of options available. Johnson and Kaplan added another option, ABC, to the possibilities on offer but seemed unimpressed with the possibility that companies might (a) accept that costing was only useful for stock valuation, (b) adopt more sophisticated (traditional) absorption costing, or (c) adopt direct or marginal costing systems. In the light of this survey it seems that few companies adopt ABC; some companies (Apple Aeros, Apricot Aeros) adopt absorption costing based on many absorption rates; and a number of companies employ variants of direct/marginal costing in their financial reporting.

Our conclusion is that the relevance lost thesis gives insufficient weight to the work of the early "absorption costers" or the later "direct costers" and overemphasises the power of ABC to solve the costing problems in some companies in the 1980s. Our study has demonstrated that companies now have a number of costing options open to them and that they select widely from these.

Recommendations

10.1   Introduction

Final recommendations chapters of reports often present "best practice" in the format of checklists of techniques or an agenda of procedures to be adopted. We have resisted such an approach. This is not merely through diffidence about advising practitioners how they should behave, though there are clearly dangers when academics who are not currently, or in some cases have never been, engaged in practice begin to instruct those who are. Nor is it ultimately because of concern over the question of: "best for whom?" although we have noted that historically any strong advocacy of particular accounting systems has soon become the target for abuse by objectors who support other forms of accounting. Rather, our rejection of the "best practice" approach is firmly rooted in the theoretical and empirical positions developed in this report.

The notion that one particular set of practices may stand as the universal template for accounting has long been rejected. Even where it is possible to identify associations between accounting practices and key "independent" variables – size, ownership, production technology, information technology – there remain considerable variations between companies. Further, should companies actually face identical circumstances, their different histories and cultures would mediate in the selection of accounting practices. Combining all such "structural" elements would be so complex that it would be impossible for an outside observer to predict what forms of accounting would fit such circumstances.

It is in the face of such complexity that the reflexive monitoring of practice by knowledgeable and skilful actors becomes important. Not only are they faced with a range of particular circumstances, and employed in companies with particular histories and cultures, but they also have to respond to managers who differ in terms of education, experience and preferences. It is within this field of opportunities and constraints that practitioners exercise "agency" in designing, proposing, implementing and changing accounting systems. It is therefore entirely in keeping with the position we have laid out in this report that this final chapter should advance not guidelines to "best practice", but rather some issues which have been raised in the study which, in our view, may be helpful in informing the reflexive monitoring of practice by practitioners and researchers.

The next section advances some suggestions for practitioners. Some of these stem from the *prevalence* of forms of accounting in survey companies. Many survey companies are satisfied with "contribution accounting" as a means of communicating financial information. The targeted use of standard costing and variance analysis is consistent with the limited extent of variance analysis reported and the telling critique of variances in the literature. Limited apportionment of overhead and activity-based analysis is consistent with the sparing use of these methods in survey companies and the standard textbook critiques of these practices. Some suggestions are based on *deductive logic*, so that, for example, *if* it is decided that contribution style, marginal costing statements are to be adopted *then* it seems logical to construct them in an efficient, technically sound and informative manner. There are examples of impressive implementation of particular practices that can be used as models by other companies. Thus the next section hopes to enable learning by combining the experience of practitioners and our analysis of this.

The final section offers some suggestions for the development of research in this area. We point to methodological issues, highlight some particular topics that might be pursued in other research, and suggest the development of international studies of innovation that will provide a comparative understanding of the development of accounting practices.

10.2   Changing practices: Issues for reflection

Simple financial reporting

In general we feel that manufacturing companies have tended to opt for relatively straightforward approaches to their routine reports. Several companies identify actual costs incurred, writing off overhead as a period expense or appearing to do so while making a simple adjustment for overhead value in stock. Often only limited and focused variance analysis is undertaken and bonus schemes employ unsophisticated measures.

The use of simple systems is most obvious in companies like Elm Engineering, Thyme Tanneries, Larkspur Lighting, Tulip Tyres, Marigold Medical and Forget-me-not Foam where our interviewees could articulate the reasons for the systems adopted. We were persuaded by the combination of prudence and common sense that these interviewees displayed in opting for conservative (marginal) costing of stock and contribution style formats. The majority of survey companies adopt contribution style statements and this provides further evidence of their efficacy.

Marginal costing and contribution analysis

If a marginal cost style format is adopted, then we would advise that either the advice of David Solomons (1965: 111) or the procedures adopted in Tulip Tyres are considered. Solomons recommended that profit be ascertained on a marginal cost basis and then an adjustment be made so that "absorption cost profit" as required by external reporting standards could also be reported. This need not be very complicated:

> It is unnecessary to make a detailed allocation of actual period costs to products for the purpose of this adjustment. All that is required for the determination of profit is to calculate what proportion of the period expense in total is applicable to the change in inventory which occurred during the period.

Tulip Tyres follows Solomons' advice but employs a full cost system in parallel with its marginal cost–based reporting and this system provides the means of valuing stock and thus generating the "whole cost adjustment" posted each month. The difference between Solomons' proposal and Tulip Tyres practice is simply in the degree of sophistication in the calculation of the monthly adjustment.

Although some companies do not make the adjustment to convert "marginal cost profit" into "absorption cost profit" every month, for companies that carry significant stock it may make sense to do this. Directors do not like to be surprised by unexpected adjustments to reported profit at the year-end!

Given that relatively simple adjustments can be made to adjust the value of stock from a marginal to an absorption basis we suggest that the stock valuation accounting standard be ignored in deciding which system should be employed for internal reporting. This point becomes increasingly important with the introduction of an international accounting standard that will mandate the valuation of stock on an absorption basis. Companies might be tempted to adopt this as perceived "best practice" in their internal reporting.

Limited use of standard costs and variances

Many survey companies employ standard costs but they calculate and report variances selectively. It seems important to identify those variances that really matter and to target their use carefully. While material and labour variances can be important in some companies there is little enthusiasm, in the survey companies, for fixed overhead volume variances. In absorption costing companies these might be necessary in accounting reconcilations but that seems to be the limit of their usefulness.

The limited and targeted use of variances would go some way to meeting Brimson's scathing attack on certain traditional practices (see Figure 2.5).

While most companies use only a limited subset of variances there were examples of companies increasing the sophistication of variance analysis by, for example, extracting the variance due to exchange rate movement from material price variances and the variance due to method changes from labour efficiency variances. For some companies such refinements might be worthwhile.

Routine reporting of profitability for key elements of the business

Contribution style reporting lends itself to analysis of the "contribution" generated by product groups, market segments, distribution channels, etc. These analyses are undertaken in several survey companies and seem very useful. Where an organisation can be structured so that its marketing organisation is matched to targeted market sectors then the contribution style analysis and attribution of marketing overhead to sectors seems particularly appropriate. We were impressed during the early stages of the project when questions oriented towards pricing and market analysis unearthed these analyses in the pilot companies.

Sparing apportionment of overhead

Some companies apportion overhead to business sectors and, in some cases, this was judged to be valuable. However, in general, "contribution companies" aim to allocate overhead only if it can be clearly attributed to markets, products, etc. Where overhead is apportioned down to net profit our interviewees were aware of the dangers of attributing real meaning to the segmental profit so derived.

More open attitudes to budgeting

In general the survey companies have institutionalised, top management driven, budgeting processes. Comparison of actual results against budget reaffirms the importance of budgeting in many companies. There seems to be little recognition of the "beyond budgeting" criticisms of traditional techniques in the survey companies and, given the logical nature of these criticisms, we suspect that more open attitudes on the uses and problems of budgeting would be beneficial.

Systematic use of forecasting and trend analysis

There is plenty of evidence of systematic forecasting in the survey companies although the focus of forecasts is often limited to the current financial year. More than half the survey companies also compare current results with those from the previous year. One company, Flax Fans, has experimented with graphical presentations that combine historical results with forecasts to the end of the *next* financial year. This company has broken the shackles of periodic annual financial reporting by ensuring that forecasts are always for one to two years ahead. The practices adopted by Flax Fans are set out in some detail in the Appendix on CDROM.

At Flax Fans, elements of cost as a percentage of sales are routinely reported and this has become an important control mechanism aimed at ensuring that target profit as percentage of sales is achieved. This sort of analysis was noted in a few other companies, providing a check that margin figures were within "acceptable" or tolerable ranges.

Companies employ a number of "reality checks", comparing current to previous year, budget and forecast results; checking for abnormalities in cost:sales ratios and using variance analysis to signal trends. All these devices seem eminently sensible and, additionally, we think the use of moving averages and graphical presentations, as at Flax Fans, has much to recommend it.

Limited use of activity-based costing

None of the survey companies were using ABC when they were interviewed although some interviewees had experience of the technique. There were examples of valuable insights gained from ad hoc activity-based analyses but there was also scepticism about the benefits that might be derived from the extensive work involved. Where companies have significant overhead and complexity in their production, distribution or marketing operations, ABC might yield useful insights. However, it seems that the technique can only be recommended if there is specific reason for its employment.

Management and executive bonus schemes

We were surprised by the extensive use of bonus schemes for management and executives. It is very difficult to judge whether these have the desired motivational impact and this seems to be a fruitful area for further research. The schemes described have a heavy emphasis towards financial indicators and, given the publicity that "scorecards" have received in the 1990s, this is surprising. Perhaps companies could consider a wider range of performance indicators in their incentive schemes than is evident in this survey.

Avoidance of spurious overhead allocations in service industry

Relatively few of the survey companies employ absorption costing systems and those that do still use traditional (not activity-based) overhead absorption bases. The apportionment of non-manufacturing overhead to cost objectives is limited. In view of the sparing use of sophisticated theory in the survey companies we are cautious of the use of this theory in the service and public sectors.

Much management accounting theory, from absorption costing to ABC, has been generated from experience in manufacturing industry – yet this theory is used sparingly in the survey companies. This suggests that service sector concerns should reflect carefully before adopting apparent "best practice" management accounting theory based on experience in manufacturing. We would advise non-manufacturing organisations to be particularly wary of the extensive use of overhead apportionments and ABC.

10.3   Research implications

Methodology

The method developed in this research might be termed *document-based interviewing*, combining scrutiny of key documents and interviews with those responsible for their construction and interpretation. The method falls between large-scale questionnaire surveys and intense field research producing case studies and thus reflects a balance between the strengths and weaknesses of each.

The strengths of postal questionnaires are facilitation of large-scale data gathering, amenability to sampling design and statistical analysis and therefore a claim to be "representative" of current conditions. However, they have several drawbacks. First, questions might not address the issues faced by practitioners. Second, the language of the questioner may not correspond with that of the questionee creating confusion on both sides. Third, even given shared language, the respondent might interpret questions differently from that intended. Fourth, the respondent might answer according to their perception of the "correct" answer instead of according to their actual practice. Fifth, postal questionnaires are not conducive to eliciting narrative answers where these would be useful. Sixth, postal questionnaires do not allow immediate cross checking of answers or follow-up of particularly interesting responses. Overall, postal questionnaires may be useful where terms are well understood and practices readily identified, especially if combined with other methods such as initial interview pilot studies and/or follow-up telephone or field interviews. But in explorations of emergent practices, with idiosyncratic terminology, the method has important inadequacies that may result in misleading findings.

In contrast the strengths of field research/case studies are the production of "rich picture" descriptions of accounting practices, their contexts, their development, their use, and their meaning for accountants and non-accountants. However, the time-consuming nature of such studies means that only a small number of sites can be visited. There is usually little opportunity for sampling (with the researcher grateful for any access granted), and though claims may be made for "validity" the cases cannot be claimed to be representative of wider trends. The approach may also be seen as overly subjective as the researcher influences not only the interpretation of the fieldwork, but also the research site itself – for example, by posing questions not previously raised in the organisation (though this could also be true of questionnaires).[36]

Standing between these research styles, document-based interviewing can address issues in a structured but informal style. Subjectivity during interviews is mediated by documentary evidence that both informs the interview and stands as an artefact external to the researchers' perceptions of it. The publication of such documents also allows the reader to assess the evidence. Of course, a price is always paid with any methodological choice. Early commitment is needed through requiring the disclosure of corporate information and, as companies may be wary of providing this, response rate is likely to be low. Once access has been achieved, the method is labour intensive: in interviewing, transcribing, summarising and analysing the results obtained. Thus, while permitting wider coverage than case study research (in this study 41 sites) the several hundred cases that may be achieved in questionnaire research is unlikely. Conversely, although interviewing facilitates understandings not available through questionnaire work, limiting interviews to one person in each company cannot expose the complex social relations that emerge in field research.

Overall, it is our view that the method proved its worth by unearthing the considerable terminological issues involved in studying costing and financial reporting systems. There were

---

[36]Although the "subjectivity" of field research may (possibly) "distort" findings, we believe that this can also be a strength. The personal skills of researchers in interrogating respondents and gaining empathy with their perspectives constitutes a research craft that can considerably enhance the process of research.

several examples where our interviewee would not have understood our definition of a term like "contribution" and, without being able to study the P&L and ask further questions we would not have understood respondents' use of terms like "gross margin", "manufacturing margin" or "direct profit". Thus the method was of very considerable value in assuring the quality of data gathered.[37]

Our study suggests a number of methodological avenues for further research. First since *documentary-based interviewing* is not a standard method in accounting research we suggest that other researchers consider its use; there may be many areas of study where an interrogation that inter-relates interviewee and documentation is valuable. Second, in the study of contemporary practice, this exploratory study may have clarified issues to the extent that they are now amenable to wider examination through *questionnaire surveys*. Third, we may have raised particular issues that are now better explored in depth through *field research*. Fourth, having now gained a clearer view of the range of practices currently observable in manufacturing, researchers may wish to use the study as a resource in conducting *longitudinal study* of accounting practice that was not possible before due to lack of reliable information.

Issues

We hope that our study has thrown up a number of issues that researchers will find intriguing and will provoke further research. Some issues point to emergent possibilities, for example, that the harmonisation process for international accounting standards will incline companies to concentrate on absorption costing and that this will compromise, if not halt, the development of marginal/direct costing in the way that SSAP9 appeared to do in the 1970s (Dugdale and Jones, 2003). Or perhaps the management accounting practices we have observed are now so strongly established that companies will run parallel systems, supported by

---

[37]We have found this in previous field research. For example, in studying investment appraisal, access to pro forma appraisal forms considerably assisted our understanding of the processes involved. However, this is the first study where we have made documentation a requirement during data gathering thus allowing comparability across all cases.

readily available and better-understood computer systems in order to maintain the usefulness of management information.

Other issues we still find perplexing. Take budgeting, for example. There are suggestions in the report that budgets are to be seen as "optimistic" or "aspirational"; whereas, in contrast, forecasts are viewed as (more) "realistic". And yet it is usual in our companies to use the budgets, and not the forecasts, for performance measurement. Further, it is performance against budget that is preferred in determining managerial bonuses. A simplistic reading suggests that companies/divisions/departments will appear to under-perform and managers will earn low (or no) bonuses. This does not seem to be the case. We can speculate about what may be going on below the superficial appearance of budgeting, but more evidence is required to understand the processes involved (and perhaps to shed light on the question of why so few companies in this survey are interested in the "beyond budgeting" movement).

On a theoretical note, this study has reinforced a suspicion that we have harboured for some time; that accounting change may demonstrate some of the life-cycle properties of a "natural history". We have observed companies that are adopting accounting systems at the same time that others are abandoning them; and accountants simplifying systems at the same time that others are making theirs more sophisticated. What we suspect, and what we advance as a very tentative hypothesis, is that our observations intervene at different stages of a cycle in different companies; that they cut through different parts of a similar pattern of change. Such a cycle, we hypothesise, might look like this:

1. introduction of a "new" system,
2. operationalising the system,
3. developing the system to make it "more sophisticated",
4. continued development of the system leads to it being re-defined from "more sophisticated" to "too complicated",
5. simplification of system,
6. dissatisfaction with existing system and reiteration of Step 1 with different "new" accounting system.

If such a cycle existed, then nature and age of accounting innovation identified by research would be a function of the moment in the cycle when the researcher entered (see Jones and Dugdale,

2002, for similar comments related to the development of ABC). For the moment these thoughts are mere speculation. It might be possible, however, to explore this possibility in future research – with longitudinal studies seeming the most promising.

International comparisons

Much of this report has emphasised the difference between companies. However, it is very likely that there is also a lot in common because the researcher and the respondent share the same taken-for-granted assumptions about the nature of business life. One dimension of this is that it is difficult for British researchers, interviewing British accountants, to disentangle the influence of the British economy, polity, society and culture on the observed accounting practices. Here, what we may take for granted in UK studies may appear unfamiliar, even unimaginable, in manufacturing companies in other countries. In particular, accounting practices that are commonplace in the UK, though they may be shared with the US and other English-speaking countries, may be very different from those experienced in the rest of Europe and elsewhere in the world.

We identify a number of assumptions that might be challenged if a more global perspective was adopted:

◆ that accounting information is a very important part of management information and central to decision-making and control;
◆ relatively large numbers of trained and qualified accountants are available to produce it;
◆ these accountants are produced by and are members of various professions that have significant self-regulatory powers;
◆ financial accountancy is the historically superior occupational wing of profession in relation to management accountancy;
◆ financial accounting information is the dominant form of external corporate information, and this is because owners primarily want information on profit.

We suggest that study of other European countries, or those further afield outside the Anglo-American sphere of influence, indicates that these are not universally applicable assumptions. In taking them for granted we fail to appreciate how much accounting innovation may be structured by the national characteristics, and associated forms of reflexivity, of the countries in which it takes place. Different countries may have different forms of innovation. Conversely, in the modern world, there may be forces of globalisation that are increasing the similarities between countries. Research in other countries not only explore into questions about such globalising forces, but also give greater insight into the nature and conditions of change in the UK.

References

Accounting Standards Steering Committee (1972) "Stocks and work in progress: Exposure draft 6", reprinted in *Management Accounting*, 158–164.

Accounting Standards Steering Committee (1975) "Statement of Standard Accounting Practice 9: Accounting for stock and long-term work in progress".

Ahmed, M. N. and Scapens, R. W. (2000) "Cost allocation in Britain: Towards an institutional analysis", *European Accounting Review*, 9 (2), April (5), 159–204.

Ahrens, T. (1997) "Strategic interventions of management accountants: Everyday practice of British and German brewers", *European Accounting Review*, 6 (4), 557–588.

Anthony, R. N. (1989) "Reminiscences about management accounting", *Journal of Management Accounting Research*, 1 (Fall), 1–20.

Armstrong, P. (1995) "Why do accountants write plays about direct costing?", *Advances in Public Interest Accounting*, 6, 1–18.

Armstrong, P. (2002) "The costs of activity-based management", *Accounting, Organizations & Society*, 27 (1), 99–120.

Ask, U. and Ax, C. (1992) "Trends in the Development of Product Costing Practices and Techniques – A Survey of Swedish Manufacturing Industry", *15th Annual Congress of the European Accounting Association*, Madrid, Spain.

Berry, A. J., Cullen, J., Seal, W. B., Ahmed, M. and Dunlop, A. (2000) *The Consequences of Inter-Firm Supply Chains for Management Accounting*, Chartered Institute of Management Accountants, London.

Bigg, W. W. (1950) *Cost Accounts* (6th edition), Macdonald and Evans, London.

Black, M. L. and Eversole, H. B. (1946) *A Report on Cost Accounting in Industry*, Government Printing Office, Washington D. C.

Bost, P. J. and Cooper, R. (1990) "Bridgeton industries automotive component and fabrication plant", reprinted in Cooper, R. and Kaplan, R. S. (eds) (1991) *The Design of Cost Management Systems*, Prentice Hall, New Jersey.

Boyns, T. (1998) "Budgets and budgetary control in Britain to c.1945", *Accounting, Business and Financial History*, 8 (3), 261–301.

Boyns, T. and Edwards, J. R. (1997a) "British cost and management accounting theory and practice", c.1850–1950, *Business and Economic History*, 26 (2), 452–462.

Boyns, T. and Edwards, J. R. (1997b) "The construction of cost accounting in Britain to 1900: The case of the coal, iron and steel industries", *Business History*, 39 (2), 1–29.

Bright, J., Davies, R. E., Downes, C. A. and Sweeting, R. C. (1992) "The deployment of costing techniques and practices: A UK study", *Management Accounting Research*, 3, 201–211.

Brignall, S., Fitzgerald, L., Johnston, R. and Markou, E. (1999) *Improving Service Performance: A Study of Step-change Versus Continuous Improvement*, CIMA, London.

Brimson, J. (1987) "CAM-I Cost management systems project" in Capettini, R. and Clancy, D. K. (eds), *Cost Accounting, Robotics, and the New Manufacturing Environment*, 5.1–5.34 American Accounting Association, Sarasota, Florida.

Burlingame, L. J. (1979) "Production and inventory control techniques as they help and are helped by finance (a case study)", *The Fourteenth European Technical Conference Proceedings*, The British Production and Inventory Control Society, 5–15.

Carter, R. N. (1938) *Advanced Accounts*, Pitman and Sons, London.

Chappell, H. P. (1978) "Developing a real time production control system – A case study", *The Thirteenth European Technical Conference Proceedings*, The British Production and Inventory Control Society, 55–62.

Church, A. H. (1917) *Manufacturing Costs and Accounts*, McGraw-Hill Book Company, New York.

Church, A. H. (1901) "The proper distribution of establishment charges", *Engineering Magazine*, July: 508–517.

Clark, J. M. (1923) *The Economics of Overhead Costs*, The University of Chicago Press, Chicago, Illinois.

Coates, J. B. and Longden, S. G. (1989) *Management Accounting: The Challenge of Technological Innovation*, Chartered Institute of Management Accountants, London.

Coneron, P. (1978) "MRP and real life", *The Thirteenth European Technical Conference Proceedings*, The British Production and Inventory Control Society, 63–78.

Cooper, R. (1988a) "The rise of activity-based costing – Part one: what is an activity-based costing system?" *Journal of Cost Management*, Summer, 45–54.

Cooper, R. (1988b) "The rise of activity-based costing – Part two: When do I need an activity-based costing system?", *Journal of Cost Management*, Fall, 41–48.

Cooper, R. (1989a) "The rise of activity-based costing – Part three: How many cost drivers do you need and how do you select them?", *Journal of Cost Management*, Winter, 34–46.

Cooper, R. (1989b) "The rise of activity-based costing – Part four: What do activity-based costing systems look like?", *Journal of Cost Management*, Spring, 38–49.

Cooper, R. (1990) "Cost classifications in unit-based and activity-based manufacturing cost systems", *Journal of Cost Management*, Fall, 4–14.

Cooper, R. and Kaplan, R. S. (1988a) "How cost accounting distorts product costs", *Management Accounting* (US), April, 20–27.

Cooper, R. and Kaplan, R. S. (1988b) "Measure costs right, make the right decisions", *Harvard Business Review*, September–October, 96–103.

Cooper, R. and Kaplan, R. S. (1991) "Profit priorities from activity-based costing", *Harvard Business Review*, May–June, 130–135.

Cooper, R. and Kaplan, R. S. (1992) "Activity-based systems: Measuring the costs of resource usage", *Accounting Horizons*, September, 1–13.

Cooper, Weiss and Montgomery (1985) "Schrader Bellows (A-E), Harvard Business School Cases 186-050/1/2/3", reprinted in Cooper, R. and Kaplan, R. S. (eds) (1991), *The Design of Cost Management Systems*, Prentice Hall, New Jersey.

Crowcroft, P. K. (1985) "MRP in the food industry", *The Twentieth European Technical Conference Proceedings*, The British Production and Inventory Control Society, 78–84.

DeCoster, D. T. (1988) "Institutional furniture", reprinted in DeCoster, D. T., Schaffer, E. L. and Ziebell, M. T. (eds) (1988) *Management Accounting: A Decision Emphasis* (4th edition), Wiley, New York.

Dent, J. (1990) "Strategy, organization and control: Some possibilities for accounting research", *Accounting, Organizations and Society*, 15 (1/2), 3–25.

Dixon, S. (1966) *The Case for Direct Costing*, The General Educational Trust of the ICAEW, London.

Drury, C. (1984) *Cost and Management Accounting* (1st edition), Van Nostrand Reinhold, Wokingham.

Drury, C. (1996) *Management & Cost Accounting* (4th edition), Thomson Learning, London.

Drury, C. (2000) *Management & Cost Accounting* (5th edition), Thomson Learning, London.

Drury, C. and Tayles, M. (2000) *Cost System Design and Profitability Analysis in UK Companies*, Chartered Institute of Management Accountants, London.

Drury, C., Braund, S., Osborne, P. and Tayles, M. (1993) *A Survey of Management Accounting Practices in UK Manufacturing Companies*, ACCA Research Paper, Chartered Association of Certified Accountants, London.

Dugdale, D. and Jones, T. C. (1997) "How many companies use ABC for stock valuation? A comment on Innes and Mitchell's questionnaire findings", *Management Accounting Research*, 8 (2), 233–240.

Dugdale, D. and Jones, T. C. (2003) "Battles in the costing war: UK debates, 1950–1975", *Accounting Business & Financial History*.

Dugdale, D., Jones, T. C. and Seward, C. (2003) *Locating Investment Appraisal in the Capital Budgeting Process*, European Accounting Association, Seville.

Edis, D. C. (1965) "Standard marginal costing in action – a case study part II", *Management Accounting*, March, 92–101.

Elbourne, E. T. (1914) *Factory Administration and Accounts*, Longman, London.

Friedman, A. L. and Lyne, S. R. (1997) "Activity-based techniques and the death of the bean counter", *European Accounting Review*, 6 (1), 19–44.

Garcke, E. and Fells, J. M. (1887) *Factory Accounts: Their Principles and Practice*, Crosby Lockwood and Son, London (4th edition reprinted, 1976 by Arno Press).

Garcke, E. and Fells, J. M. (1893) *Factory Accounts: Their Principles and Practice*, Crosby, Lockwood and Son, London.

Garner, S. P. (1954) *Evolution of Cost Accounting to 1925*, University of Alabama Press, Alabama.

Glover, G. R. and Williams, R. G. (1928) *Elements of Costing*, The Gregg Publishing Company, London.

Goldratt, E. M. (1990) *The Haystack Syndrome*, North River Press, New York, September, 329–332.

Goldratt, E. M. and Cox, J. (1984) *The Goal*, Gower, Aldershot.

Graham, D. and Harris, F. T. P. (1984) "Distributed inventory management", *The Nineteenth European Technical Conference*

Proceedings, The British Production and Inventory Control Society, 114–127.

Harris, J. N. (1936) "What did we earn last month?", *N.A.C.A. Bulletin*, January, 15.

Harrison, G. C. (1930) *Standard Costs: Installation, Operation and Use* The Ronald Press Company, New York.

Hazell, W. H. (1921) *Costing for Manufacturers*, Nisbeth, London.

Hendricks, J. A. (1988) "Applying cost accounting to factory automation", *Management Accounting* (USA), December, 24–30.

Holzer, H. P. and Norreklit, H. (1991) "Some thoughts on the cost accounting developments in the United States", *Management Accounting Research*, March, 3–13.

Hoolihan, J. B. S. (1978) "MRP and the organisation", *The Thirteenth European Technical Conference Proceedings*, The British Production and Inventory Control Society, 103–116.

Hopper, T., Kirkham, L. Scapens, R. and Turley, S. (1992) "Does financial accounting dominate management accounting – a research note", *Management Accounting Research*, 3, 307–311.

Horngren, C. T. (1962) *Cost Accounting: A Managerial Emphasis*, Prentice Hall Inc., Englewood Cliffs, N.J.

Horngren, C. T., Foster, G. and Datar, S. M. (1996) *Cost Accounting: A Managerial Emphasis* (9th edition), Prentice Hall International, New Jersey.

ICAEW (1960) "Recommendation on Accounting Principles No. 22: Treatment of Stock-in-Trade and Work in Progress in the Financial Accounts", reprinted in *Accountancy*, November, 1960, 633–638.

Innes, J. and Mitchell, F. (1990) *Activity Based Costing: A Review with Case Studies*, Chartered Institute of Management Accountants, London.

Innes, J. and Mitchell, F. (1995a) "A survey of activity-based costing in the U.K.'s largest companies", *Management Accounting Research*, June, 137–154.

Innes, J. and Mitchell, F. (1995b) "ABC: A follow up survey of CIMA members", *Management Accounting* (UK), 73/7, July–August, 50–51.

Innes, J. and Mitchell, F. (1997) "Survey research on activity-based costing: a reply to Dugdale and Jones", *Management Accounting Research*, June, 241–249.

Innes, J., Mitchell, F. and Sinclair, D. (2000) "Activity-based costing in the U.K.'s largest companies: A comparison of 1994 and

1999 survey results", *Management Accounting Research*, September, 11 (3), 349–363.

Johnson, H. J. and Kaplan, R. S. (1987) *Relevance Lost: The Rise and Fall of Management Accounting*, Harvard Business School Press, Boston, Massachusetts.

Johnson, H. T. and Loewe, D. A. (1987) "How Weyerhauser manages corporate overhead costs", *Management Accounting* (US), August, 20–26. Reprinted in Cooper, R. and Kaplan, R. S. (1991) *The Design of Cost Management Systems: Text, Cases and Readings* (1st edition). Prentice Hall, New Jersey, pp. 575–580.

Johnson, H. T. (1992) *Relevance Regained: From Top-down Control to Bottom-up Empowerment*, The Free Press, New York.

Jones, T. C. (1992) "Understanding management accountants: The rationality of social action", *Critical Perspectives on Accounting*, 3 (3), 225–257.

Jones, T. C. and Dugdale, D. (2001) "The concept of an accounting regime", *Critical Perspectives on Accounting*, 12 (1), 35–63.

Jones, T. C. and Dugdale, D. (2002) "The ABC bandwagon and the juggernaut of modernity", *Accounting, Organizations & Society*, 27 (1), 121–163.

Joseph, N., Turley, S., Burns, J., Lewis, L., Scapens, R. and Southworth, A. (1996) "External financial reporting and management information: A survey of U.K. management accountants", *Management Accounting Research*, 7, 73–93.

Kaplan, R. S. (1985) "Accounting lag: The obsolescence of cost accounting systems", *California Management Review*, 28 (2), 174–199.

Kaplan, R. S. (1987) "Regaining relevance", in Capettini, R. and Clancy, D. K. (eds), *Cost Accounting, Robotics, and the New Manufacturing Environment*, 7.1–7.29 American Accounting Association, Sarasota, Florida.

Kaplan, R. S. (1988) "One cost system isn't enough", *Harvard Business Review*, January–February, 61–66.

Kaplan, R. S. (1998) "Innovation action research: Creating new management theory and practice", *Journal of Management Accounting Research*, 10, 89–118.

Kilvington, K. W. (1974) "Has the management accountant emerged far enough and fast enough?" *Management Accountant*, December, 324–328.

Kuhn, T. S. (1962) *The Structure of Scientific Revolutions*, University of Chicago Press, Chicago.

Kuhn, T. S. (1970) "Reflections on my critics", in Lakatos, I. and Musgrave, A. (eds) *Criticism and the Growth of Knowledge*, Cambridge University Press, Cambridge.

Lawrence, F. C. and Humphreys, E. N. (1947) *Direct Costing*, MacDonald and Evans, London.

Lawrence, P. and Lorsch, J. (1947) *Organization and Environment*, Harvard Business School, Division of Research, Boston.

Lee, R. S. (1981) "MRP and the organisation", *The Fourteenth European Technical Conference Proceedings*, The British Production and Inventory Control Society, 77–85.

Lilly, R. T. (2001) *The Road to Manufacturing Success: Common Sense Throughput Solutions for Small Business*, St Lucie Press, Boca Raton, Florida.

Loft, A. (1986) "Towards a critical understanding of accounting: The case of cost accounting in the U.K., 1914–1925", *Accounting Organizations and Society*, 11 (2), 137–169.

Loft, A. (1990) *Coming into the Light*, CIMA, London.

Longman, D. R. and Schiff, M. (1955) *Practical Distribution Cost Analysis*, Homewood, Richard D. Irwin, Illinois.

Luscombe, M. (1993) *MRPII: Integrating the Business*, Butterworth-Heinemann, Oxford.

Mackison, G. (1981) "How to extend MRP into product costing and the benefits to the business which result", *The Sixteenth European Technical Conference Proceedings*, The British Production and Inventory Control Society, 129–139.

March, A. and Kaplan, R. S. (1987) "John Deere Component Works, Harvard Business School Case 187-107/8", reprinted in Cooper, R. and Kaplan, R. S. (eds) (1991) *The Design of Cost Management Systems*, Prentice Hall, New Jersey.

Matthews, D. R. (1961) "Treatment of stock-in-trade and work in progress in financial accounts", *The Cost Accountant*, February, 52–53.

Middleton, K. A. (1968) "Standard costing overhead variances", *Management Accounting*, Feb, 60–67.

Miller, P. and O'Leary, T. (1993) "Accounting expertise and the politics of the product: Economic citizenship and modes of corporate governance", *Accounting, Organizations and Society*, 18 (2/3), 187–206.

Mitchell, F. and Walker, S. P. (1997) "Market pressures and the development of costing practice: The emergence of uniform costing in the U.K. printing industry", *Management Accounting Research*, 8, 75–101.

NAA (1961) "Current application of direct costing", *N.A.A. Research Report* 37, National Association of Accountants, New York.

NACA (1953) "*N.A.C.A. Bulletin No. 23 Direct Costing*", National Association of Cost Accountants, New York.

Noreen, E., Smith, D. and Mackey, J. T. (1995) *The Theory of Constraints and its Implications for Management Accounting*, The North River press, Great Barrington, MA.

Quail, J. M. (1996) "Proprietors and Managers: Structure and technique in large British enterprise 1890 to 1939", PhD thesis, University of Leeds.

Robinson, M. A. (ed.) (1990) "Contribution margin analysis: No longer relevant/Strategic cost management: The new paradigm", *Journal of Management Accounting Research*, 2, 1–32.

Roslender, R. and Hart, S. (2001) *Marketing and Management Interfaces in the Enactment of Strategic Management Accounting Practices*, CIMA Publishing, London.

Roxburgh, J. G. (1983) "Integrated manufacturing and accounting", *The Eighteenth European Technical Conference Proceedings*, The British Production and Inventory Control Society, 147–160.

Ryan, R. and Hobson, J. (1985) *Management Accounting: A Contemporary Approach*, Pitman, London.

Sandretto, M. J. (1979) "Paramount Cycle Company, Harvard Business School Case 180-069", reprinted in Cooper, R. and Kaplan, R. S. (eds) (1991) *The Design of Cost Management Systems*, Prentice Hall, New Jersey.

Scapens, R. W. (1991) *Management Accounting: A Review of Recent Developments* (2nd edition), Macmillan, London.

Scapens, R., Turley, S., Burns, J., Joseph, N., Lewis, L. and Southworth, A. (1996) *External Reporting and Management Decisions*, CIMA, London.

Sizer, J. (1963) "Marginal costing – caution!", *The Cost Accountant*, March, 86–88.

Sizer, J. (1973) "Accountant's contribution to data collection, solution control", *Management Accounting*, February, 49–52.

Smith, D. (2000) *The Measurement Nightmare: How the Theory of Constraints Can Resolve Conflicting Strategies, Policies, and Measures*, St Lucie Press, Washington.

Solomons, D. (1950a) "Uniform costing – A survey Part I", *Economica*, May, 237–253.

Solomons, D. (1950b) "Uniform costing – A survey Part II", *Economica*, November, 386–400.

Solomons, D. (ed.) (1952) "The historical development of costing", in *Studies in Costing*, Sweet and Maxwell, London.

Solomons, D. (1965) *Divisional Performance: Measurement and Control*, The research foundation of Financial Executives Institute, New York.

Thompson, J. S. (1958) "What a works manager expects from his cost accountant", *The Cost Accountant*, June, 12–15.

Vollmers, G. L. (1996) "Academic cost accounting from 1920–1950: Alive and well", *Journal of Management Accounting Research*, 183–199.

Wheldon, H. J. (1937) *Cost Accounting and Costing Methods* (4th edition), MacDonald and Evans, London.

Wilson, R. M. S. (1999) *Accounting for Marketing*, International Thomson Business Press, London.

Wilson, R. M. S. and Chua, W. F. (1988) *Managerial Accounting: Method and meaning*, Van Nostrand Reinhold (International) Co Ltd, London.

Witham, R. M. (1985) "Making MRP work in the pharmaceutical industry", *The Twentieth European Technical Conference Proceedings*, The British Production and Inventory Control Society, 96–100.

Subject Index

Author Index